INSIDE:

As the mass slaughter rages on in Gaza and now Lebanon, and tensions ramp up exponentially in Ukraine, the US held its quadrennial kayfabe wrestlemania spectacular that vaunts itself as a democratic presidential election. This edition chronicles Trump's win as he yet again became the befittingly ugly face of the increasingly ugly empire.

All works are written by Caitlin Johnstone and Tim Foley. The Caitlin Johnstone project is 100 percent reader-funded.

Visit caitlinjohnst.one for the original articles and their supporting links.

You Can Only Support Trump Or Harris If You Don't See The US Empire For The Beast It Is
•Notes From The Edge Of The Narrative Matrix•

People who think of either Donald Trump or Kamala Harris as decent or acceptable simply have not realized how immensely evil you have to be to become a US president.

In order to support either Harris or Trump you need to have an extreme ignorance of the murderousness and depravity of the US empire, which they both serve. Only a complete failure to see and understand the vast scale of the abusiveness of the US power structure could cause you to view these two candidates as meaningfully different from each other — let alone see one of them as decent enough to be worthy of your support.

Both Trump and Harris are auditioning for a role that will necessarily entail the creation of mountains of human corpses by US-sponsored violence, as has every viable US presidential candidate throughout our lives.

This is because the US empire is deeply evil. Not the country called the United States in and of itself, but the globe-spanning power structure which functions as an empire that's structured around it. This vast power structure is held together by rivers of human blood, and if you're the Democratic or Republican nominee to lead it as president then you are necessarily a deeply evil person, because you have sufficiently assured all the necessary powers that be that you will continue that bloodshed in order to become the nominee.

Most Americans (and most westerners generally) fail to truly see and understand how profoundly evil the US-centralized empire is, which is the only thing that allows all this political energy to go into pretending there are these hugely significant differences between the Democrat and the Republican presidential candidate every four years. If they could really ingest the scale of the empire's brutality and tyranny with a deep sense of empathy for their fellow human beings upon whom it is inflicted, they would never support anyone who is pledged to help operate the slaughter machine, and they would not see any would-be operators of that machine as meaningfully different from any other. All they would see is the need for the slaughter machine to be dismantled.

The most sophisticated propaganda engine ever created exists to prevent this understanding from taking root, in the west generally and in the United States in particular. Americans are the most propagandized population on this planet, and their propaganda indoctrination is at its most intensive during the quadrennial performance ritual known as the US presidential race. The whole thing is geared toward falsely exaggerating the differences between the two candidates while drawing emphasis away from the 99 percent of the issues on which they are indistinguishable from each other. And those 99 percent similarities happen to be on all the most murderous and tyrannical behaviors of the US government.

If Americans weren't so aggressively propagandized and indoctrinated, this would all be obvious to them, and this election race performance wouldn't get them clapping along

like children at a puppet show. The abusive status quo necessary for maintaining the US-centralized empire would not be consented to at all, and would be forced to collapse. There's too much power riding on preventing this from happening for Americans to be allowed to have a real say in their elections, so they are propagandized to the gills into clapping along instead.

•

Liberals are freaking out because The Los Angeles Times and The Washington Post chose not to endorse a presidential candidate this election cycle, which is silly. Newspapers shouldn't endorse political candidates. How is this not obvious to everyone?

It's absolutely ridiculous that news outlets endorsing political candidates is a thing at all. The first job of a real journalist is to have an adversarial relationship with those in power, regardless of who wins. The only correct political position from the perspective of journalistic ethics is "If you are in power I will do everything I can to expose all your lies and misdeeds, no matter what your party or platform happens to be." This position is vastly more important in the US, the nation with the world's most powerful government, and becomes more important the more influence your news outlet has.

If you are campaigning for one side or the other, you've obviously hurt your ability to take this position. You're communicating a line of favoritism not only to the public, but to your outlet's staff, and to the politicians you're meant to be holding to account. You're making decisions which can help or hinder your outlet's ability to gain access to an administration once in office by doing or not doing what amounts to a political favor for them. The press should not be doing political favors for any political candidate, and the expectation that they should inhibits their ability to do critical journalism.

Obviously news outlets have biases like anyone else, and they should do everything they can to bring transparency to those biases. But that should look like saying "Yes we have an ideological bias, so here's what we're doing to prevent that from skewing our coverage of the powerful," not "Everybody please vote for Candidate X because we like them more than Candidate Y."

The whole controversy is stupid. The LA Times and Washington Post shouldn't be endorsing a presidential candidate. No news outlet should, at least if they purport to be engaged in journalism rather than political activism.

•

Back when people used to watch TV they'd complain that there's "a hundred channels and nothing on," and they were right: there WAS nothing on that was worth watching. Mainstream culture was just that vapid and worthless — and it still is. There's nothing in it that fulfills us, that nourishes us in the ways we long to be nourished, that tells us real things in a real way about the world as it actually is. People would flip through TV channels disgusted at the emptiness of it all because that's all they were being presented with: empty drivel with no edifying or transformative value.

People experience the same thing today when scrolling through their online media feeds and streaming services. They're searching for something true and meaningful, but unless you've been lucky enough to stumble into a rare corner of the internet where real things are being discussed, all the algorithm feeds you is propaganda and distraction. Mindless entertainment. Celebrities. Gossip. Mainstream electoral politics. Donald Trump.

For generations we've been corralled toward streams of information which are designed to turn us into idiots and sociopaths. Designed to keep us from getting good information about what the powerful people who rule us are really up to. To dull our curiosity and keep us from asking useful and penetrating questions about our society. To direct any political impulses we might be able to muster in this confusing fog toward mainstream political factions which all support the status quo. To stop us from looking too closely at the death and misery our government inflicts upon people in far away countries. To keep us from noticing that we live in a mind-controlled dystopia that is fueled by endless exploitation, abuse, mass military violence, and ecocide. To keep us mindlessly turning the gears of the empire and trusting our rulers to sort things out on our behalf. To keep us sedated and compliant instead of brilliant and inconvenient.

It takes work to get outside of that matrix of manipulation. It takes time to find good sources of information and ingest what they've got to teach us. It takes effort to find our way into depth and meaning inside this fraudulent empire. But that's what we all ache for. That's what kept people flipping through channels in frustration in the glory days of television. They were looking for the depth. They were searching for something authentic. Something real.

Forming a truth-based relationship with reality can be difficult, but it's a necessary step if you want to be an authentic person and come out of that itching sense of dissatisfaction which all controlled minds must inevitably experience. This is the only path to real and lasting happiness. Until then all you get is the fake decoy happiness they try to sell you in advertisements and Hollywood movies that comes from always getting your way and owning the right products and achieving all your goals and having a compelling personal story to tell people. This isn't real happiness. It cannot last. It cannot satisfy.

Only truth can lead to satisfaction. And everything in this fake plastic dystopia is structured around preventing us from ever finding it.

Featured image via U.S. Indo-Pacific Command (CC BY-NC-ND 2.0)

The West Only Has Pretend Heroes Like Spider–Man And SpongeBob

As the US-backed atrocities in the middle east get uglier and uglier, I keep thinking about something that was said by an Iranian cleric named Shahab Moradi after the US assassinated Iran's immensely popular general Qassem Soleimani in 2020.

Moradi complained that Iran can't even really retaliate for the assassination because the US doesn't have any real heroes of its own like Soleimani, saying, "Think about it. Are we supposed to take out Spider-Man and SpongeBob?"

I've never seen a more incisive and withering critique of western culture, and I probably never will. It's such an accurate statement and paints such a clear picture of what this civilization is really like that it's hard to imagine how anyone could possibly top it.

There are no real heroes with popular support in the western empire, because everything that's truly heroic gets stomped down here, and everything that gets amplified to popularity is either vapid distraction or directly facilitates the interests of the evil empire.

Our own generals are busy butchering civilians for oil and geostrategic control.

Our military personnel are imperial stormtroopers.

Our police are the security guards of capitalism.

Our most prominent journalists are all propagandists.

Our most prominent celebrities are famous because of their ability to pretend to be fictional characters doing fake things in Hollywood movies.

Our most prominent artists are famous because of their ability to churn out formulaic pop songs about empty-headed bullshit.

Our most widely recognized symbols are corporate logos.

Our most highly regarded professionals are those who can sell westerners the most future landfill manufactured by wage slaves in the global south.

Our most well-known government leaders are those who've sold their souls to oligarchs and imperialists and can lie to the public most convincingly.

The only westerners doing truly heroic things here get thrown in prison, or murdered, or pushed into obscurity, because the only truly heroic thing anyone can do in today's world is to take a stand against the western empire.

Those who bravely resist the US war machine or make themselves inconvenient for western empire managers don't get to become popular heroes. You don't see the westerners who work to stop weapons shipments to Gaza being celebrated for their efforts on CNN and the BBC. You don't see antiwar activists getting Hollywood movies made about their work — at least not until the wars they were protesting lie safely in the distant past. You don't see journalists who work to expose the most egregious crimes of the empire being elevated to fame and fortune.

The only figures who get elevated to fame and fortune in this fake plastic dystopia are those who either actively serve the interests of the empire or who passively distract people from its abuses. Donald Trump. Elon Musk. The Kardashians. Taylor Swift. Spider-Man and SpongeBob.

Those are the only heroes we're allowed to have here in any major way. You can have real heroes if you want, but if you tell the average westerner their names the first word out of their mouth will be, "Who?"

Every once in a great while someone will sneak past the many security checkpoints into fame and begin opposing the empire, but they are always quickly demonized and marginalized by the imperial perception managers. And for every Roger Waters or Susan Sarandon, there are a thousand imposter heroes making themselves extremely convenient for the rulers of the western empire.

This is the civilization we live in. A mind-controlled wasteland where everything is fake and stupid. The only path toward fulfillment and inner peace in such a dystopia is to dedicate yourself to tearing it down, brick by plastic brick.

Featured images via Inside the Magic (CC BY-NC-ND 2.0) and Joshua Roberts/Pexels.

Yeah, Yeah, UNRWA Is Hamas. Everyone Israel Hates Is Hamas.
•Notes From The Edge Of The Narrative Matrix•

The Israeli Knesset has banned UNRWA, an absolutely critical agency for getting humanitarian aid into Gaza, with the architect of the bill saying this was happening because "UNRWA equals Hamas".

In addition to everything else this genocide has been, it's been a colossal insult to our intelligence. UNRWA is Hamas. Hospitals are Hamas. Journalists are Hamas. Civilian infrastructure is Hamas. Ambulances, schools and mosques are Hamas. The women and babies — okay maybe they're not technically Hamas, but Hamas is definitely hiding behind them and using them as human shields.

We are asked to believe self-evidently idiotic things, and if we don't, we get called Nazi Jew-haters. We are being asked to turn ourselves into empty-headed morons to advance the information interests of a foreign state that's allied with our government. Stupidity is being framed as a sign of patriotism. Gullibility is being framed as a sign of rejecting antisemitism. In this morally bankrupt and perverse civilization, the noblest thing you can be is a blithering imbecile.

•

Axios and its Israeli intelligence insider Barak Ravid have penned yet another White House press release disguised as a news story about how "concerned" the Biden administration is about Israel's actions in Gaza.

"The Biden administration is 'deeply concerned' that two bills passed by the Israeli Knesset on Monday will exacerbate the already dire humanitarian crisis in Gaza and harm Palestinians in East Jerusalem and the West Bank," Ravid writes.

Oh shit you guys the Biden administration is deeply concerned that Israel is doing something bad in Gaza! You're in trouble now, Bibi!

Like I said. Just one nonstop insult to our intelligence.

•

CNN has issued an apology after its panelist Ryan Girdusky told fellow panelist Mehdi Hasan "I hope your pager doesn't go off" after Hasan said he supports Palestinians. Israel supporters have been directing this "hurr hurr you should be murdered with an explosive pager" wisecrack at Israel's critics for weeks, and apparently Girdusky just forgot where he was in the heat of the moment.

CNN was like, This network is shocked and appalled that our panelist joked about murdering a British Muslim journalist with an explosive beeper. That kind of language is only appropriate when directed at Muslims who live in the middle east.

•

Per the rules of the western empire you are a religious extremist if you want to fight against an occupying force who has been abusing you your entire life, but you are not a religious extremist if you want to carpet bomb the middle east to help fulfill a Biblical prophecy.

•

MSNBC's Rachel Maddow is back to pushing her "Russians are interfering in the US election" narrative, so we know what we'll be hearing again if Kamala loses. No matter who wins we can expect a bunch of outraged shrieking from the other side that the election was unfairly stolen from them.

The US presidential race is very openly a contest between two oligarch-owned Zionist war whores, and yet after the results are announced next week you're still going to hear half the country going "OMG election interference! The election was stolen from us!"

It already was, you dopes. It was stolen before the race even started. The rest is just narrative.

•

I sure hope all the US progressives who obediently stopped talking about Gaza these last couple of months remember to start that thing up again after the election is over.

•

I'm just gonna say this ahead of time so it's out there: you don't get to campaign on continuing a genocide and then blame other people when you lose. That is not a thing.

•

"Trump will be worse on Gaza" is such an obnoxiously dishonest argument. It's completely unfalsifiable and can't even be tested after the election since abuses keep getting worse in Gaza anyway, and it's based on nothing but the claim that very vague statements made by Trump prove he'll facilitate Israeli atrocities more than the current administration already has been. It's completely empty narrative fluff with no basis on the facts in evidence.

There are all kinds of legitimate cases to be made that Harris would be a little bit better than Trump on some aspects of domestic policy and the environment, but there is no case whatsoever to be made that he'll be worse on Gaza than the administration that's already committing genocide there. He could be worse, he could be a bit better, or he could be exactly the same. There's no way to know, and there won't be any way to know in a universe where we can't observe alternate realities to compare what each presidential candidate would have done if they'd won. It's an entirely unanswerable question that people are just pretending to know the answer to.

Harris and the Democrats have repeatedly attacked Trump for not starting a war with Iran when he was president. She criticized him for making John Bolton sad when he refused to bomb Iran. How is that less insanely pro-Israel than anything Trump has said?

If you want to argue that Harris will be better on reproductive rights or something then go ahead, but when it comes to Gaza don't piss on my leg and tell me it's raining.

Featured image via Adobe Stock.

"Too Much Evidence" Of Genocide

South Africa's legal team has submitted hundreds of documents containing what it calls "undeniable evidence" as part of its ongoing genocide case against the state of Israel, with the South African representative to The Hague telling Al Jazeera that "The problem we have is that we have too much evidence."

The Israeli outlet Haaretz reports that IDF soldiers are actively blocking the return of Palestinians they have driven out of northern Gaza as part of the so-called "General's Plan" — a land grab of Palestinian territory using ethnic cleansing by violent force.

Haaretz has been far more critical of Israel's actions than western media outlets have been. It recently published an editorial titled "If It Looks Like Ethnic Cleansing, It Probably Is". Haaretz publisher Amos Schocken is now publicly advocating international sanctions on the Israeli government for its apartheid abuses and opposition to a Palestinian state, drawing an outraged response from the Netanyahu regime.

Last week there was a two-day rally attended by multiple Israeli government officials called the "Preparing to Resettle Gaza Conference," which was exactly what it sounds like: high-profile Israelis gathering to discuss the agenda to drive Palestinians out of the Gaza Strip and replace their territory with Jewish settlements.

Humanitarian aid in Gaza has reportedly fallen to its lowest level since Israel's genocidal onslaught began, with just a few hundred truckloads entering the enclave from October 1 to October 22 and nothing getting through to the north. The UN's Under-Secretary-General for Humanitarian Affairs recently warned that "The entire population of North Gaza is at risk of dying," a warning that was issued shortly before the Israeli Knesset voted to cut off UNRWA aid throughout all the territories it controls.

According to a new report from The Washington Post, the US State Department has been inundated with hundreds of reports of US-supplied weapons being used to needlessly kill and harm civilians in Gaza, but in violation of its own rules it has failed to take any action on a single one of them. According to one WaPo source, investigations of these reports have tended to stall out at the "verification" stage, which consists of asking the Israeli government for its side of the story.

Israeli forces reportedly killed 109 Palestinians in a single massacre on Tuesday — including dozens of children — when Israel blew up an apartment building where hundreds of civilians were sleeping.

The IDF killed five journalists in a single day last Sunday, bringing the total number of journalists murdered in Israel's genocidal assault to at least 180. This occurred shortly after Israel published a kill list of six Al Jazeera journalists who it claims are secret Hamas fighters, although no Al Jazeera reporters were among the five killed.

And this is just in Gaza. Israel has already killed some 164 healthcare workers in its ongoing assault on Lebanon, where the Netanyahu government is sabotaging ceasefire negotiations by inserting ridiculous non-starter demands like Israeli planes being allowed to enter Lebanese airspace and Israeli forces being allowed to police the ceasefire deal with military operations in southern Lebanon as they see fit.

Every day there's more and more ugly news in the middle east, perpetrated by Israel and its powerful western backers who make its abuses possible. It's getting harder and harder to stay on top of. There really is "too much evidence" to keep up with.

Featured image via Adobe Stock.

Vote However You Feel; This Whole Show Is About Feelings Anyway

My one and only position on how Americans should vote is that they should do whatever makes them feel nice, since that's all US presidential elections are: an emotional pacifier to let the masses feel like they have some meaningful control over their country. It's about feelings and nothing else.

If voting for Kamala Harris makes you feel nice because it lets you pretend you're stopping fascism or protecting women and minorities or helping to secure a ceasefire in Gaza or whatever, then go right ahead. That's what your vote is there for.

If voting for Donald Trump makes you feel nice because it lets you pretend you're sticking it to the establishment or punishing the Democrats for their misdeeds or ending the wars or whatever, then by all means do so. This whole spectacle is exclusively about feelings.

If voting for a third party makes you feel nice because it lets you pretend there might be some answer in electoral politics or that the empire will ever allow anyone who truly opposes the abuses of capitalism, militarism and imperialism anywhere near power, then get in there and cast that vote. Whatever makes your feely bits feel nice.

Just don't make the mistake of thinking you're doing anything other than sucking on an emotional pacifier, because you're not.

No matter how you vote, Democrats will continue to win approximately half the time, and Republicans will win the other half.

No matter how you vote, the ever-expanding abuses of capitalism and plutocracy will continue making life worse for ordinary Americans.

No matter how you vote, the US war machine will continue inflicting nightmarish mass military violence on people in other countries in order to maintain its globe-spanning empire.

No matter how you vote, the profit-driven systems which rule our world will continue exterminating our biosphere at an alarmingly rapid rate.

No matter how you vote, the empire's looming confrontations with Russia and China guarantee more world-threatening nuclear brinkmanship in the near future.

No matter how you vote, people in the global south will continue to be robbed and exploited to give the western citizenry of the imperial core enough cheap stuff to keep them pacified and compliant.

No matter how you vote, the US will continue using starvation sanctions, blockades and economic warfare to bully weaker nations into obedience.

Your rulers will never give you the tools to end any of these abuses, because too much power rides on their continuation. They will only give you the tools to mollify your own frustrations and placate your discontentment by giving you a phony ritual to participate in every four years that lets you feel some degree of control.

You're never voting your way out of this. The oligarchs and empire managers who rule you are never going to let you overthrow them by ticking a box. These sociopaths are never going to give their power to you voluntarily out of the kindness of their hearts.

Their rule will end when the project of the US empire ends — either because of outside forces beyond their control, because of inside forces beyond their control, or some combination of these two factors. It

will not come about because of how anyone voted in any November. It will only happen because it was forced to happen.

You can help force this to happen by working to foment a revolutionary zeitgeist within your country. You can do this by helping to wake up as many of your countrymen as possible to the fact that their government and media are lying to them constantly, that everything they've been taught about their nation and their world is false, and that a better world is possible.

Lies and propaganda play an enormous role in holding the imperial power structure together, so the most effective way to help bring it down is by spreading truth and awareness. Show people how they're being lied to, abused and stolen from. Teach them the truth about the wars, about their government, about their media, about their nation, about the people their government has designated as enemies, and about the abusive systems they all live under.

That's real action. That kind of work matters. Your vote doesn't matter beyond its ability to help you feel a certain way. So do whatever you need to do to feel how you want to feel on election day, and then go do some real work.

Featured image via Adobe Stock.

How To Go On In A World Full Of Cruelty

One of the most common questions I get asked tends to go something like, "How do you go on? How do you keep looking at all the cruelty in this world and writing about it every day? Don't you ever get overwhelmed? Don't you ever want to give up in despair? What keeps you going, day after day?"

And the truth is the ugliness does overwhelm me sometimes. The first really graphic image I saw of a child's body ripped apart in Gaza last year stopped me dead in my tracks. I just went limp and crumbled onto the couch and didn't move for hours.

And I do quit sometimes. I quit hard. I quit with everything I've got. Sometimes things look very dark and I cast my laptop aside and say "That's it, no more, I quit" with every fiber of my being and go lie down. I give myself over to the feelings and to the overwhelm and the despair, and I quit.

I quit struggling, I surrender fully to the feelings, and I let them say everything they want to say without interruption or mitigation. And then when they've had their say and gone quiet, I get up, and I pick up my laptop, and I get back to work.

That's really it. I don't have any special stories in my head that give me hope. I don't think about the bright spots of goodness in this world or the heroic actions of noble individuals to motivate me. I don't read the works of great thinkers or listen to the words of great speakers to reignite the spark. I just feel it all, all the way through, and go on.

It's not hope that keeps me going, it's love. Love for this beautiful planet and all the weird little critters scuttling around on it, especially the fingery ape monsters walking about on their hind legs making mouth noises about their mind noises. I love this whole chaotic wondermess so very, very much, and I want it to keep going.

It really is so insanely beautiful. All of it, not just the sweet photogenic parts that make us feel sweet photogenic feelings.

There is immense beauty even in the black smoke coming from Gaza.

There is immense beauty even in dead birds.

There is immense beauty even in deforestation.

There is immense beauty even in the whales starving to death with bellies full of plastic.

There is immense beauty even in coal mines.

There is immense beauty even in factory farms.

There is immense beauty even in the seediest parts of town.

There is immense beauty even in the most murderous empire managers.

There is immense beauty even amid the ugliest atrocities.

It's always there. If you can't see it, it's because you're not looking closely enough. Beauty is just a word for the experience of having truly seen something.

That's what keeps me going, no matter how ugly things get. Because even in the ugliness, there is immense beauty. Even in the grief. Even in the anger. Even in the waves of sadness. Beauty is always present.

It's not hard to keep going once you have realized that everything has beauty. No matter how dark things get, you still get to dance this exhilarating dance on this strange little blue marble spinning through space, and you still get to work to make sure that future generations get to dance too.

This work doesn't have to be miserable. It has to be sorrowful at times, frustrating at times, scary at times, downright enraging at times, but it never needs to be miserable. Learn to perceive the beauty in all that arises and you'll find not only the will to fight, but a clear reason to keep on fighting for as long as your body draws breath.

Featured image via EU Civil Protection and Humanitarian Aid (CC BY-NC-ND 2.0).

The Mainstream Western Worldview Pretends The Global South Does Not Exist

Mainstream western politics and culture pretend the rest of the world does not exist. The mainstream western worldview shrinks the earth down to US-aligned countries and acts as though the billions of people who live in the global south do not share a planet with us.

You really see this illustrated in US presidential election season, when debates will feature five or six minutes on "foreign policy" with the remaining two hours dedicated to "domestic policy" and culture war wedge issues despite the the White House's relationship with foreign countries having orders of magnitude more significant real-world consequences. Americans discuss election results as though the whole thing revolves around them and their feelings and how much more convenient or inconvenient the next president might make their lives, while Europeans discuss what the results might mean for NATO expenses and trade agreements. The fact that the next US president will be committing genocide, starving people with economic sanctions and increasing Washington's stranglehold on earth's population by any amount of violence and tyranny necessary barely ever enters into the conversation.

Whenever you hear western officials talking about how "the international community" views a particular issue, they're almost always talking about the US, Canada, Europe, Australia, and maybe a few US-aligned Asian countries like Japan and South Korea — while pretending the rest of the world just isn't there.

You see it in politics, but you see it throughout our culture too. In our movies, our shows, our conversations, our thoughts. We don't really think about all the exploitative imperialist extraction of resources and labor that makes our lifestyles possible, even though it directly affects damn near every waking moment of our lives. You wouldn't be reading this sentence right now had not this exact dynamic led to a highly complex electronic device making its way into your field of vision.

We just conduct ourselves from moment to moment like this relationship isn't happening. It's as though we're all walking around with living people strapped to our feet like slippers, but we're just laughing and talking about the weather and celebrities and how we're feeling about this and that without ever acknowledging the existence of the human beings we're standing on top of.

The global south is omitted from our thinking and our conversations in this way all the time, leaving us in this fractured, redacted mental universe where we pretend we're the only people living in this rapidly shrinking world. Our lives are no less significant or valuable than those of people in Africa or Asia, but we live as though they don't exist, even when their labor may affect our moment to moment reality far more than the white-skinned person we're paying attention to in this instant.

This is going to have to change if we're to become a conscious species and create a healthy world together. Our perception of the world is going to have to reflect the actual world, not just the small cloistered segment which exists within the confines of western civilization. We're going to have to start thinking about humanity as a whole and stop living the lie that we are not intimately interconnected with the lives on every populated continent.

Until we open up our worldview and begin taking into account the needs and struggles of our fellow human beings around the world, it will be like we're at a dinner party that's being waited on by slaves. We're all looking at each other and talking about our lives and our families as the slaves clear our plates and refill our drinks, never acknowledging them or discussing the fact that they're being kept as material property and forced to do what they're doing to avoid punishment and torture. Until we demand their freedom and invite them to come and dine with us, we're going to be in a highly dysfunctional and abusive relationship with them, and nothing will ever feel quite right — because it won't be.

•

Gaza Tells Us Who We Are

Some days it's hard to say which is more horrific: the Gaza genocide itself, or the moral decay throughout our society which makes it possible.

I mean, the atrocities in Gaza have a couple million victims. If you add up the populations of the US, Europe, Canada and Australia, you've got around a billion people living in a dystopia whose collective conscience is so warped and twisted that they'd allow their governments to support a live-streamed genocide in full view of the entire world. A billion people who are so morally bankrupt that they find it tolerable for such a nightmare to be inflicted upon their fellow human beings right in front of them.

This has been especially pronounced during the heat of a US presidential race, with tens of millions of voters falling all over themselves to cognitively sweep Gaza under the carpet so they can throw their support behind one of the two mainstream candidates who've both pledged to support the Zionist state which is perpetrating this genocide. At best they see Israel's crimes as an annoying side issue which the left keeps disrupting their Kamala parties about, and at worst they support Israel's actions entirely.

What a pointless, meaningless, soulless way to live. What a betrayal of truth, and of our own humanity. How could anyone possibly find satisfaction in that kind of zombie-like existence? Mindlessly shuffling along to the beat of the status quo, devouring human flesh because it's more comfortable than the cognitive dissonance which would come with divorcing the power-serving worldview you've been indoctrinated from birth into espousing.

I was listening to an interview with a doctor who worked in Gaza during the genocide and he discussed the time many months ago when the IDF forced the evacuation of a hospital and left four premature babies to die in their incubators after assuring the staff they'd be taken care of. Their tiny bodies were found decomposing weeks later after Israeli forces cleared out of the area.

How did that one incident, just by itself, not stop the world? How did it not stop us all in our tracks and force us to re-evaluate everything that led to this point? It wasn't a secret that those four babies died; it was in the mainstream news. It was right there, right in front of us, and we did nothing.

Such atrocities have been happening on a daily basis for thirteen months now, and still nothing.

We've got to live like this. We've got to live in this genocidal dystopia, surrounded by shambling sleepwalkers covered in human blood. Our lives here in the west are far, far more comfortable than the lives of people in Gaza, but they are also far less truthful, and far less capable of nourishing the human spirit.

We marinate in lies and psychopathy, watch lies and psychopathy, eat drink sleep and breathe lies and psychopathy. Our minds are full of garbage and our hearts are full of shit, and we are wading around up to our ankles in the blood, sweat and tears of the global south. This festering sore of a civilization is the only soil in which the western-backed genocide in Gaza could take root.

The people in Gaza have to suffer the consequences of who we are and what we have become, but we have to live with who we are and what we have become. We're killing their babies and leaving them to rot, but we're the ones who have to live with the corpses of rotting babies in our souls.

One way or another the killing in Gaza will end one day. But the forces within us which gave rise to that butchery will live on long after the sounds of the drones and explosions have ceased.

We will have to live like that. We will have to live knowing that this is who we are.

Featured image via Wikimedia Commons/Farsnews.ir (CC BY 4.0)

The Evil Warmongering Zionist Won (No Not That One, The Other One)

The Democratic Party has lost control of both the White House and the Senate. As of this writing it is still unclear which party will secure control of the House of Representatives. Turns out campaigning on the promise of continuing a genocide while courting endorsements from war criminals like Dick Cheney is not a great way to get progressives to vote for you.

One interesting point is that Donald Trump appears to have taken the battleground state of Michigan, where Kamala Harris was soundly rejected by the large Arab American population of Dearborn despite their voting overwhelmingly for Biden in 2020. Back in August, Harris famously shushed Muslim anti-genocide protesters at a campaign rally in Michigan by admonishing them with the words "I'm speaking".

Well, who's speaking now?

To be clear, this is not a good result. A good result was not possible this election. The warmongering Zionist genocide monster lost, which means the other warmongering Zionist genocide monster won.

Donald Trump is still bought and owned by Adelson cash, which means we can expect him to be just as much of a groveling simp for Israel as he was during his first term. The president elect has publicly admitted that when he was president the Zionist plutocrats Sheldon and Miriam Adelson were at the White House "probably almost more than anybody" asking him to do favors for Israel like moving the US embassy to Jerusalem and acknowledging Israel's illegitimate claim to the Golan Heights, which he eagerly did.

Trump closed out his campaign tour alongside his former CIA director and secretary of state Mike Pompeo, which should be enough to dash the hopes of even the most naive Trump supporters that US foreign policy is headed in a positive direction in January. As CIA director, Pompeo led a plot to assassinate Julian Assange and cheerfully admitted that "we lied, we cheated, we stole" at the agency. This odious swamp creature has remained in Trump's good graces for the last eight years, and is reportedly expected to have a position in Trump's cabinet once again.

Speaking at a campaign event in Pittsburgh on Monday, Pompeo boasted that he has been called "the most loyal cabinet member to Donald J Trump" and said that when Trump is re-elected "we will take down the ring of fire; we will support our friends in Israel." The "ring of fire" is think tank speak for Iran and the militias in Lebanon, Iraq, Syria, Yemen and Palestine who oppose Israel.

So things are probably going to get uglier and uglier. But they were getting uglier and uglier under Biden, and they would have gotten uglier and uglier under Harris as well. That's just what it looks like when you've got a dying empire fighting to retain planetary control like a cornered animal. You don't get to be the US president unless you are willing and eager to do ugly things.

Democrats exaggerate how destructive Trump is relative to their own bloodthirsty psychopath candidates. While we can expect Trump to inflict tyranny and abuse upon Americans, it will be nothing compared to the tyranny and abuse he's going to inflict on people in other countries, and it will be nothing compared to the tyranny and abuse his predecessor has been inflicting on people in other countries. All the histrionic shrieking we see from US liberals about Trump only works inside a western supremacist worldview that does not see the victims of US warmongering as fully human, and therefore sees scorched earth genocidal atrocities as less significant than comparatively minor abuses concerning US domestic policy.

Abandon hope that any positive changes will come from this election result.

Abandon hope that Trump will do good things.

Abandon hope that Democrats will learn any lessons from this loss.

Abandon hope that liberals will suddenly remember that genocide is bad and start protesting against the US-backed slaughter in Gaza.

Abandon hope in US election results, period.

US elections do not yield positive results. They are not designed to benefit ordinary human beings.

Nothing changes for those of us who are dedicated to fighting against the abuses of the US empire. It will be the same fight after January 20 as it was on January 19.

We fight on.

•

Oh No, Now The US Will Have A President Who Does Bad Things
•Notes From The Edge Of The Narrative Matrix•

So hey, can Democrats finally start opposing genocide now?

Just kidding. They won't.

•

Democrats are sitting on a mountain of hundreds of thousands of human corpses they helped kill by mass military slaughter in the last four years, weeping and lamenting that now bad things are going to start happening.

•

Democrats are shrieking so loud today because they know they're wrong. They know their party ran a dogshit candidate. They know it was crazy to expect the left support the party that's committing a live-streamed genocide.

It's not anger.

It's not fear.

It's cognitive dissonance.

•

I should probably repeat what I said back in July: if you're a Trump supporter who started reading me for my criticisms of the Biden administration, you are going to hate my guts after your guy gets in.

•

Democrats will spend the next four years viciously attacking Trump. So will I. But while Democrats will attack Trump because of the few ways in which he is different from themselves, I will be attacking him because of the many ways in which he is the same as the Democrats.

Both parties are in full alignment when it comes to the worst evils of the US empire. I and others like me will be focusing there, while the Democrats pour all their energy into pretending to be a real opposition party and exaggerating the differences between themselves and Trump.

•

The reason US presidential elections are so close and US politics remain divided pretty much 50-50 is because both parties are constantly walking the tightrope of trying to give the donor class as much as possible while giving Americans as little as possible and still getting votes. As soon as they figure out they can make fewer concessions to ordinary voters and still have a chance at winning, they roll back those concessions to make concessions to the plutocrats who own them.

They're constantly calculating how little they can get away with giving the voting public. Give too much to the people and the plutocrats switch sides; give too little and the people won't vote for you. So they both walk it right up to the line year after year, keeping them split right down the middle and never changing the status quo in any major way.

Which just so happens to be exactly what the rich and powerful oligarchs who own America want.

•

The only real solution to the trolley problem is to find and kill the prick who keeps tying people to trolley tracks and making people choose which ones die.

•

A leftist is someone with logically and morally correct politics. A liberal is someone who wants to feel logically and morally correct without ever putting themselves at odds with power or costing themselves opportunities or experiencing the uncomfortable emotions that truth causes.

•

Meanwhile, Israel keeps brutally hammering Lebanon and Gaza with the full support of the United States. The Israeli military has publicly announced that the Palestinians who've been driven out of northern Gaza will not be allowed to return to their homes, meaning that this is a completely undisguised ethnic cleansing operation.

Benjamin Netanyahu fired Yoav "We're exterminating human animals" Gallant on Tuesday because he's too moderate and gentle for the current Israeli government. He has been replaced by the even nastier Israel Katz, who said in 2022, "Yesterday I warned the Arab students, who are flying Palestine flags at universities: Remember 48. Remember our independence war and your Nakba, don't stretch the rope too much. [...] If you don't calm down, we'll teach you a lesson that won't be forgotten."

If these things had happened after Trump was sworn in, liberals would be trying to rub it in our faces telling us it proves he's worse on Gaza. But it's happening now while they've still got a couple more months in power, so liberals are just ignoring it.

•

I honestly don't think my respect for Democrats could sink any lower. It was very low already, but watching them try to bully people into supporting a genocidal monster these last few months has dropped me to a whole new level of disgust I didn't know was possible.

Featured image via Wikimedia Commons

Donald Trump Is Not Your Friend

Virulent Iran hawk Brian Hook has reportedly been chosen by Donald Trump to help staff the State Department of the incoming administration, just in case you were still holding out hope that this time might be different and Trump really would end the wars and fight the deep state.

Readers might remember Hook as the swamp creature who in 2017 was seen in a leaked State Department memo lecturing Rex Tillerson on the US government's policy of using human rights as a cynical tool to undermine enemies and reinforce alliances. This is done, Hook explained, by ignoring human rights abuses when they are perpetrated by US allies while emphasizing them at every opportunity in the nations of enemy governments in order to "impose costs, apply counter-pressure, and regain the initiative from them strategically."

"The 'realist' view is that America's allies should be supported rather than badgered, for both practical and principled reasons, and that while the United States should certainly stand as moral example, our diplomacy with other countries should focus primarily on their foreign policy behavior rather than on their domestic practices as such," Hook wrote in the memo, saying that "In the case of US allies such as Egypt, Saudi Arabia, and the Philippines, the Administration is fully justified in emphasizing good relations for a variety of important reasons, including counter-terrorism, and in honestly facing up to the difficult tradeoffs with regard to human rights."

"One useful guideline for a realistic and successful foreign policy is that allies should be treated differently — and better — than adversaries," Hook wrote. "We do not look to bolster America's adversaries overseas; we look to pressure, compete with, and outmaneuver them. For this reason, we should consider human rights as an important issue in regard to US relations with China, Russia, North Korea, and Iran. And this is not only because of moral concern for practices inside those countries. It is also because pressing those regimes on human rights is one way to impose costs, apply counter-pressure, and regain the initiative from them strategically."

Hook's words, shared in confidentiality with the political neophyte Tillerson, were an excellent window into what western empire managers are doing when they feign outrage at alleged human rights abuses in nations they've targeted for destruction. The fact that his would be one of the first names chosen by Trump suggests we can expect more despicable foreign policy recklessness from the returning president.

I'm already getting people telling me to "give Trump a chance" and stop criticizing him before he's in office when I point out developments like this. Give Trump a chance? He had

four years. He was the president for four fucking years. Trump showed us who he is: a murderous warmongering empire lackey just like his predecessors.

The best predictor of future behavior is past behavior. There's no reason to think this time will be different. Trump criticizes foreign interventionism because that kind of rhetoric is popular, not because he actually means it. In order to get to where he's at Trump cut deals with Zionist oligarchs, powerful lobby groups, and more or less the exact same Republican voting base and donor class that's given rise to every other disgusting Republican president in recent years. Even if he wanted to end wars and fight the establishment (and there is no evidence that he does), he's already tied his own hands with the deals he's made with the powerful establishment factions he's promised his service to.

Trump supporters are George W Bush supporters LARPing as Ron Paul supporters. They act like they're backing some anti-war figure who's taking a meaningful stand against the machine, when they're really backing a guy who spent four years rolling out longstanding neocon agendas.

That's what makes them so annoying. At least liberals are more or less honest about wanting to preserve the status quo; Trumpers want you to take seriously their belief that they participated in some huge revolutionary act by ticking a box for the Republican on election day. They correctly believe that their country is controlled by an unelected deep state (though they are very confused about who that actually is), but they incorrectly believe this unelected power structure can be defeated by voting for one of the two mainstream candidates presented to them at the ballot box. Like that would ever be an option.

I am really not looking forward to another four years of that shit, I'll be honest. For four fucking years these

morons were in my mentions telling me every action of Trump's that I criticized was actually a brilliant 47-dimensional chess maneuver against the deep state, even when he was openly advancing some longstanding agenda of the CIA and neoconservative swamp monsters like ramping up aggressions against Iran or staging a coup in Venezuela. They warm up to me because they see me criticizing the media and talking about corrupt power structures and go "Ooh, she's like me!", but then they cannot understand why I keep criticizing their shitty Republican daddy figure. And then I have to spend my time explaining to them that their hero is a murderous imperialist shitstain.

And at the same time I'm going to have to be criticizing the Democrats because they'll be attacking Trump for being insufficiently hawkish on foreign policy, because that's the only foreign policy criticism you're allowed to level at a US president in mainstream politics and media — which will only contribute to the problem of Trump supporters thinking I'm on their side. It's a much less efficient and straightforward way for me to do my thing than when there's a Democrat in charge of the war machine. It's not my preferred way to operate.

Let me make things simple: if you are cheering for the US president, you are not fighting the power. You are a power-worshipping bootlicker, and you should feel embarrassed.

Your president is not your friend. The US president will always, always serve the warmongering power structure you correctly feel needs to be opposed. The plutocrats and empire managers who rule your country are never, ever going to let you vote them out of power.

Hope that helps.

Featured image via Chairman of the Joint Chiefs of Staff (CC BY 2.0)

The Air In Gaza Smells Like Corpses

The newspapers keep saying the air in Gaza smells like corpses.
Like rotting human flesh; the entire Gaza Strip.
They say it emanates from the rubble.
Pervades everything.
It's just what Gaza smells like,
like how Hershey, Pennsylvania smells like chocolate,
or how Milpitas, California smells like landfill.

I bet you can never get the smell out.
Out of your clothes.
Out of your hair.
Out of your dreams.
Out of your heart.

I bet none of us can.

Gaza smells like rotting corpses, and
our whole civilization smells like Gaza.
You walk into a Starbucks and it hits you.
You go watch Trump's inaugural address and there it is.
The smell of rotting dead children wafts from our own ruins.
Fills our minds.
Fills our nightmares.
Fills the speech of the yammering pundit.
Fills the feigned joy of the social media influencer.
Fills the light pouring from our screens onto our faces in the dark.

We can scrub as hard as we like,
but that smell's never coming out.

It will follow us straight down to hell.

Featured image via WAFA/Wikimedia Commons.

Trump Puts An Appropriately Ugly Face On A Very Ugly Empire
•Notes From The Edge Of The Narrative Matrix•

The only thing I like about Trump is exactly what so many empire managers hate about him: he gives the game away. He says the quiet parts out loud. He's the only president who'll openly boast that US troops are in Syria to keep the oil or lament that they failed to take the oil from Venezuela, or just come right out and tell everyone he's bought and owned by Zionist oligarchs.

Trump is the opposite of Obama, who was very skillful at putting a pretty face on the evil empire. Trump puts a very ugly face on a very ugly thing. He is a much more honest face to have on the empire. A crude, stupid plutocrat who is owned by other plutocrats is the perfect representative of that tyrannical power structure.

•

The propaganda machine has been spinning its head off trying to frame soccer brawls in Amsterdam as a horrifying "pogrom" against Jewish people because the side instigating the violence were supporters of team Maccabi Tel Aviv who flew in from Israel.

Video evidence shows far right Israeli hooligans terrorizing the streets of Amsterdam, chanting "Fuck the Arabs", starting fights, beating people, tearing down Palestinian flags, attacking a cab driver, and singing "Let the IDF win and fuck the Arabs! Why is school out in Gaza? There are no children left there!"

In the face of all this evidence of atrocious behavior by Israeli soccer fans, The New York Times ran a story with the headline "Antisemitic Attacks Prompt Emergency Flights for Israeli Soccer Fans". The Wall Street Journal ran with "Antisemitic Attacks in Amsterdam Prompt Tight Security at Jewish Sites". "Pogroms have returned to Europe, and the 'anti-racist' Left are silent," says The Telegraph.

Meanwhile the Daily Mail sports section ran with a headline more in line with what people actually saw: "Israeli football hooligans tear down Palestine flags in Amsterdam as taxi drivers 'fight back' in night of chaos ahead of Maccabi Tel Aviv's visit to Ajax".

Leaders of western nations like the US, UK, Canada and France joined the Dutch king in framing these soccer brawls and hooliganism as a historic mass-scale hate crime against Jews, while Israeli officials have been melodramatically shrieking like their hair is on fire.

These exhausting victim-LARPing freaks. Stop playing sports with Israel. Stop holding sporting events which could lead to the deranged members of a genocidal apartheid state showing up in your community stirring up violence and hate so they can cry victim and say you holocausted them.

Another thing that sucks about the fake "antisemitism" crisis that the western political-media class are pretending to believe in is that it will probably become a kind of self-fulfilling prophecy which creates real hatred of Jewish people.

You can't keep telling everyone over and over and over again that Jews and Israel are one and the same and that any criticism of one is always necessarily an attack on the other while the state of Israel is murdering children by the tens of thousands without contributing to unfair prejudice against Jewish people everywhere. Israel is exacerbating this effect by insisting its actions represent all Jews and are done in defense of Judaism while committing genocidal atrocities under a Star of David flag.

If you understand the truth that modern Israel is a settler-colonialist project of the western empire which uses the Jewish religion as an excuse to inflict violence and tyranny in a crucial geostrategic region, then you understand that there's no real connection between modern Israel and the Jews you encounter in your community. Sure a majority of western Jews buy into the empire's lies and support Israel, but a majority of the westerners of all faiths buy into the empire's lies about its wars and official enemies and all its other propaganda too. This is just what it looks like when you live in a highly propagandized society which is structured to psychologically manipulate people into consenting to nonstop military violence.

Once you understand this, you see that blaming ordinary Jews in your society for the actions of the state of Israel makes about as much sense as blaming ordinary Muslims for the actions of the Saudi royals — but most people don't understand this. It takes a lot of learning and close examination, and most people haven't reached that level of lucidity in our confusing information landscape which is distorted by lies and propaganda.

So when they see a self-evidently evil thing being done and hear their leaders and pundits telling them over and over again that if you hate what you're seeing then you necessarily hate Jewish people, what understanding do you think they're going to form in their minds?

Greater hatred and prejudice looks like a fairly inevitable consequence of this messaging from where I'm sitting. And it will all be the fault of the western pundits and politicians who are aggressively promulgating this message throughout our society right now in an effort to stomp out criticism of an active genocide.

•

The garment-rending emotional reaction to the US election results compared to the apathy on Gaza over the last year tells you that liberals don't see Palestinians as human beings. They'll deny it, but it's true. Their emotions show you much more than their words ever will. This is who they are.

Ignore their words and watch their actions. It works with politicians, it works with entire governments, and it works with individuals too. If you see someone flailing around on the ground because their genocidal candidate lost after spending a year walking around functioning perfectly fine throughout a year of genocide, that tells you something about them that their words would never tell you.

People are always much more honest with their actions than their words, because words can spin narratives and actions cannot. If you're ever unsure of someone's true motivations and where they really stand, don't ask them, just watch them. They'll tell you eventually, with their actions and not their words.

Featured image via Gage Skidmore (CC BY-SA 2.0)

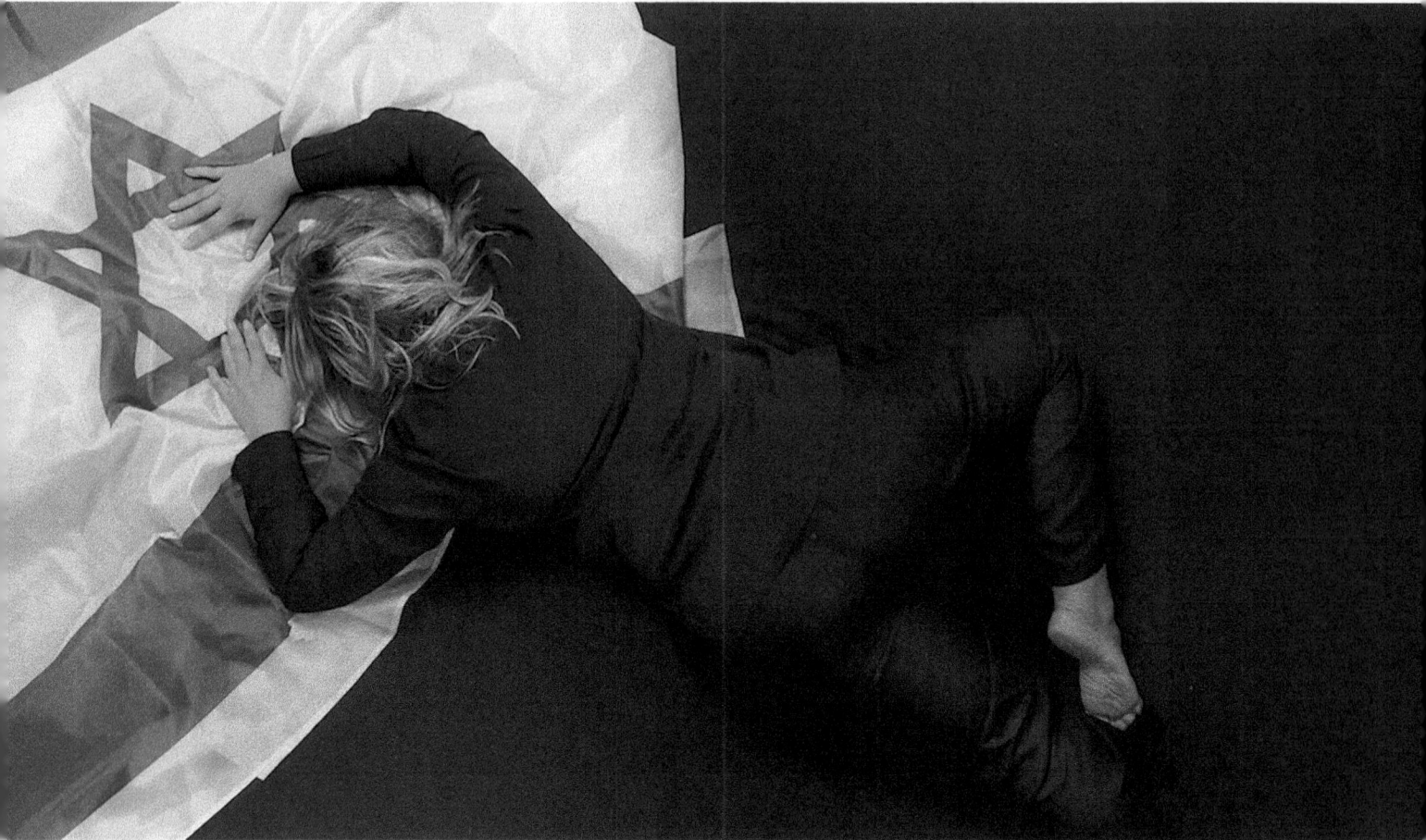

Israel Keeps Finding New Ways To Play Victim While Committing Genocide
•Notes From The Edge Of The Narrative Matrix•

Israel is really struggling with how difficult its present circumstances make playing the victim. It keeps having to invent new abuses to be victimized by like the imaginary Amsterdam "pogrom" and the fake mass rape narrative that surfaced months after October 7, because it can't sit comfortably in the role of victimizer while on trial for genocide in international courts.

Playing victim is too deeply ingrained in the narrative control strategies of Israel and its apologists, so they have to keep coming up with new and innovative ways for Israel to be victimized even when it is very clearly the last state on earth who has any business being viewed as such.

•

We keep seeing the word "pogrom" used to refer to Israeli hooligans getting their asses kicked for obnoxious behavior in Amsterdam even as Israeli settlers keep committing textbook pogroms in the occupied West Bank.

Just a week ago armed Israeli settlers went on a violent rampage torching Palestinian people's houses, vehicles and olive trees in order to terrorize them and drive them away. This is the exact type of behavior that the word "pogrom" has historically been used to describe, but you never hear that word used in the mass media to describe Israeli thuggishness. Instead we're seeing it used to describe Israeli soccer hooligans getting beat up after they tore down Palestinian flags and sang chants about murdering children in Gaza.

•

So we're seeing some good news and some bad news about Donald Trump's potential cabinet picks when it comes to US warmongering and militarism.

The good news is that Trump has publicly ruled out giving psychopathic war hawks Nikki Haley and Mike Pompeo a role in his next administration, explicitly naming them in a post on Truth Social and saying they won't be invited.

This announcement suggests that Trump is at least trying to win the favor of the more anti-interventionist faction of his base. Pundits like Tucker Carlson have been publicly crusading against both Haley and Pompeo throughout this election cycle, and I mention Carlson specifically because he reportedly has Trump's ear and was believed to have played a role in talking Trump out of bombing Iran in 2019.

The bad news is that other professional warmongers appear to be working their way into the administration. Reports from both Bloomberg and Fox News say the horrible Mike Rogers is under consideration to be the next secretary of defense. The Ron Paul Institute's Daniel McAdams has a good thread on Twitter calling Rogers "an utter warhawk neocon" who is "arguably worse than Pompeo and Rubio," noting that Rogers has promoted insanely hawkish positions on Ukraine/Russia, Israel/Iran, and China.

This news, in addition to Trump's selection of Iran hawk Brian Hook to help staff the incoming State Department, makes it clear that Trump could still easily wind up with a cabinet packed full of warmongering swamp monsters just like last time. Hopefully he keeps getting pressured not to do so.

•

In a new article on "the expanding ground occupation of the Gaza Strip by the IDF" about the way Israel has been carving up Gaza and seizing more and more territory, Israel's Ynet News reports that far right elements within the Israeli government are simply waiting for the Israeli hostages held by Hamas to die so that their deaths can be used to justify continued occupation and the construction of Jewish settlements in Gaza.

It's like a false flag conspiracy theory, except it's definitely happening and is being done right out in the open, and is even being announced ahead of time.

•

Democrats: Oh no the right wing voters we again tried to win over voted Republican again and we lost again.

Leftists: So stop doing that and win over the left instead by promoting immensely popular social policies.

Democrats: No way man, if we do that we'll lose.

Featured image via Adobe Stock.

Biden's Legacy Is Genocide, War, And Nuclear Brinkmanship

Biden's legacy is genocide, war, and nuclear brinkmanship. That's all anyone should talk about when this psychopath finally dies. Anything positive he may have accomplished in his political career is a drop in the ocean compared to the significance of these mass-scale abuses.

Biden spent his entire career promoting war and militarism at every opportunity, and then spent the twilight years of his time in Washington choosing to continue supplying an active genocide that is fully dependent on US-supplied arms.

He refused off-ramp after off-ramp to the horrific war in Ukraine that has burned through a generation of men in that country, which he knowingly provoked by amassing a military proxy threat on Russia's border in ways the US would never tolerate being amassed on its own border. In the early weeks of the conflict Biden and his fellow empire managers sabotaged peace talks to keep the war going for as long as possible with the goal of bleeding Moscow, and at one point his own intelligence agencies reportedly assessed that the probability of a nuclear war erupting on this front was as high as 50–50.

Coin toss odds on nuclear war. To call this a crime against humanity would be a massive understatement.

Biden has been facilitating Israeli atrocities in the middle east with US military expansionism in the region and bombing operations in Yemen, Iraq and Syria. He will spend his lame duck months backing Israel's scorched earth demolition of southern Lebanon.

This is who Biden is. It is who he has always been. It is true that his brain has begun to rot away like just like his conscience has rotted, but in his lucid moments he adamantly defends his administration's decisions as the only correct course of action, and it aligns perfectly with his past. To know this, one need only to look at the pivotal role he played in pushing the Iraq invasion, or his extremist rhetoric about how "If there were not an Israel we'd have to invent one."

This is the legacy that Democrats were forced to spend the last election cycle pretending is great and awesome. It's no wonder they lost. So now, as a parting gift from Joe Biden, Americans and the world get another four years of Donald Trump.

That's the story of Joe Biden. That's the whole entire thing. Anything on top of that is irrelevant narrative fluff.

Featured image via Gage Skidmore (CC BY-SA 2.0 DEED)

The Incoming Trump Administration Is Already Filling Up With War Sluts

Donald Trump has named Republican congressman Mike Waltz as his next national security advisor, a position that was held by ultrahawk John Bolton in the last Trump administration.

Like Bolton, Waltz is a warmongering freak. Journalist Michael Tracey has been filling up his Twitter page since the announcement with examples of Waltz's insane hawkishness, including his support for letting Ukraine use US weapons to strike deep into Russian territory, criticizing Biden for not escalating aggressively enough in Ukraine, advocating bombing Iran, opposing the US military withdrawal from Afghanistan, and naming Iran, North Korea, China, Russia and Venezuela as "on the march" against the United States toward global conflict. The mainstream press are calling Waltz a "China hawk", but from the look of things he's a war-horny hawk toward all the official enemies of the United States.

Trump has also confirmed that Republican congresswoman Elise Stefanik will be taking on the role of US ambassador to the UN, a role previously held by warmonger Nikki Haley in the last Trump administration. Again, there doesn't seem to be much difference between the old hawk and the new one.

Stefanik is best known for her congressional efforts to stomp out free speech on college campuses, making a lie of Trump's lip service to the importance of First Amendment rights. As explained by Antiwar's Dave DeCamp, she's a hawkish swamp monster whose political career was primed in some of the most odious neoconservative think tanks in Washington, and opposes placing any limits on US military support for Israel. Earlier this year Stefanik actually flew to Israel to give a speech before the Israeli Knesset vowing to help stop the "antisemitism" of protesters against Israel's genocidal atrocities at American universities.

And now we're getting reports throughout the mass media that deranged war slut Marco Rubio has been tapped as Trump's new secretary of state. It's really hard to imagine anyone worse for the role of Washington's top diplomat than a warmonger who has spent his entire political career pushing for more wars, sanctions and slaughter at every opportunity.

This should dash the hopes of Trump supporters everywhere that this time their guy really will end the wars and drain the swamp. Trump's appointment of Iran hawk Brian Hook to help staff the State Department for the next administration and his rumored consideration of Mike Rogers for secretary of defense are likewise bad signs, as is Tucker Carlson's claim that virulent China hawk Elbridge Colby is likely to play a role in the administration.

Trump's anti-interventionist supporters loudly applauded the other day when he unexpectedly announced that Mike Pompeo and Nikki Haley would not be playing a role in the next administration. In response to the announcement, libertarian comedian and podcaster Dave Smith said on Twitter that stopping Pompeo was not enough and that "we need maximum pressure to keep all neocons and war hawks out of the Trump administration." In response to Smith's post, Donald Trump Jr tweeted, "Agreed!!! I'm on it."

When I saw this, I tweeted the following:

"Ignore their words and watch their actions. Been saying it for years, and I'm going to keep on saying it. Ignore their words, watch their actions. Talk, as they say, is cheap."

Their actions are telling us a lot more than their words right now.

Featured image via Gage Skidmore (CC BY-SA 2.0)

To Be Pro-Israel Is To Be Pro-War
•Notes From The Edge Of The Narrative Matrix•

The way raw video evidence debunked the "Amsterdam pogrom" narrative in real time in full view of the entire world is exactly why Israel hates journalists. It's why it won't let the western press visit Gaza, and it's why it murders Palestinian journalists at every opportunity.

•

Trump's "America First" cabinet is being packed full of swamp monsters who want to pour American money into helping Israel destroy the middle east, pour American money into the unwinnable proxy war in Ukraine, and prepare American troops to fight a war with China to defend Taiwan.

•

And just as we're reacting to the news of Trump filling his new cabinet with murderous warmongers, the Biden administration comes in with a helpful reminder that they too are evil blood-soaked monsters. The White House has announced that it will be imposing zero consequences on Israel for failing to abide by its 30-day deadline to let more aide into Gaza. The "deadline" was a phony election ploy, just as we said it was at the time.

•

Friendly reminder that Biden could still end the genocide in Gaza right now. He could end it today. He could have ended it any day over the last thirteen months. Israel's atrocities will continue into the next administration because the Biden administration wants them to.

•

Everything American liberals are worried will be done to them by the Trump administration are things that were done to people in other countries by the Biden administration.

•

Anyone who supported Trump on anti-war grounds already has more than enough evidence to stop doing so. If you're still supporting him after his cabinet picks thus far you're going to support him no matter what he does on foreign policy, because you don't really care about peace — you just care about your favorite political party winning.

•

I'm already getting Trump supporters all over my replies telling me that the hawkish inclinations I'm seeing from the incoming administration aren't what they look like. They did this throughout his entire first term. Four fucking years of morons telling me the insane acts of warmongering I was witnessing were actually fine and good, or even brilliant strategic maneuvers against the deep state warmongers. Really not looking forward to another four years of this shit.

•

Being pro-Israel is being pro-war, because the state of Israel cannot exist in its present iteration without nonstop US-backed military violence. Supporting Israel necessarily means supporting endless western military interventionism in the middle east. Trump supporters keep lying to themselves about this.

It was obvious that Trump's "anti-neocon" schtick was bullshit even before his cabinet picks. You cannot be "anti-neocon" and also be Israel's BFF. That's not a thing. US military support for Israel is absolutely central to the neoconservative ideology — just research the history of neocons and PNAC. Trump and his allies talk a big game about massively unpopular Bush-era neocons, but Trump has always been fully aligned with those same neocons on Israeli warmongering. He had actual PNAC members in his cabinet like Elliott Abrams and John Bolton for fuck's sake, and he has openly admitted to being bought and owned by the Adelsons.

So the Trump faction is doing this weird cognitive dissonance straddle where they're more or less completely aligned with the neocons on middle east policy (and China policy as well for the record) while posturing as big opponents of neoconservatives and warmongers. There is a faction of the "MAGA" movement which is anti-Israel, or at least anti US aid for Israel, but they are a much smaller and far less powerful contingent. It will be interesting to see how this plays out.

•

When people defend the Gaza genocide by saying "those Arabs hate gay people" or whatever, they're admitting that they think someone having different beliefs than their own justifies wiping out their entire population.

You normally hear this argument from right wing Israel supporters speaking to left-wing Palestine supporters. They assume it's a debate-winning argument because they know leftists support LGBTQ rights, so upon hearing this the leftist will say "Oh okay well kill them all then."

Leaving aside the premise that all Palestinians hate gay people (which is of course silly), the fact that they project this assumption onto others says a lot about their own worldview. Anyone making this argument is telling you they would support the mass military slaughter of you and everyone who thinks like you if given the opportunity, because they believe those who think differently than themselves should be exterminated.

•

Leftists, liberals and rightists all mean very different things when they say they support free speech.

When an anti-imperialist socialist says they support free speech, they mean they want the freedom to hold power to account, scrutinize their government's actions, and share dissident ideas and information. This is the original reason freedom of speech has been enshrined as an important value in our society, and it's why leftists (the real kind) aggressively defend it.

When a rightist says they support free speech, they typically mean they want to be able to say racist things without any consequences and make mean jokes about trans people on social media. It's less about holding power to account and more about being able to say what you want wherever you want for its own sake, because not being allowed to say what you want doesn't feel very nice. This is what you're looking at when you see Trump talking about the importance of free speech rights while also saying he wants to jail people for burning the American flag and telling donors he'll crack down on pro-Palestine protests. He's not promising the freedom to speak truth to power, he's promising the freedom to say racial slurs.

When a liberal says they support free speech, they typically mean they support free speech for themselves and people who think like them, and for the citizens of enemy countries like Iran and China. They're more than happy to see speech critical of the powerful curbed in the name of stopping "disinformation" or "Russian propaganda". They support Silicon Valley tech platforms collaborating intimately with US government agencies to suppress dissident ideas and information, so long as doing so doesn't benefit a rival political faction. They believe their worldview is the way, the truth and the light, and that information needs to circulate in a way that helps others believe this too.

There are of course exceptions and variations on this; American libertarians are often an odd hybrid of the leftist and rightist schools of thought on free speech, for example. It's good to be aware that when someone says they support free speech, they could mean something very, very different from what you mean when you say it.

Featured image via Israel Ministry of Foreign Affairs on Flickr (CC BY-NC 2.0)

When The Show Is Over, The Actors Hold Hands And Take A Bow

President Biden and President Elect Trump met at the White House on Wednesday and shook hands and exchanged pleasantries after an emotionally exhausting presidential race in which each side accused the other of presenting an immediate existential threat to the country.

This is it. This is the real story. This image, right here.

Ignore all the fake drama. Forget all the campaign rhetoric and kayfabe conflict. This is what's real. This is what deserves your attention.

They do not hate each other. They do not see one another as an existential threat to the nation. They are not enemies. They're barely even opponents. When the show is over they hug and kiss like boxers after weeks of phony trash talk made solely to sell pay-per-views.

One may say his opponent is the next Hitler, coming to end democracy and take everyone's votes and destroy the country. The other may say his opponent is a communist dictator, come to do the same. But when the play is over the performers hold hands and bow, and then they go out and have a drink together.

They each pretend to be fighting against each other in defense of you and your interests, when in reality they're on the same side, fighting against you, in defense of the interests of oligarchy and empire.

You can see it right there. They're not hiding it anymore. They don't have to. It was all a show, and they're openly admitting it. A friendly match, like two rich ladies playing tennis at the Hamptons.

They can show it openly because they know most of you won't pay attention to what you are seeing, or if you do you'll forget all about it and get swept up in the heat of the next election cycle. There's so much messaging reinforcing the illusory partisan divide that these tacit little admissions tend to go completely overlooked.

Don't get me wrong, the depravity of Trump himself is not illusory. Real people are going to suffer and die under his administration, just as real people suffered and died under Biden's. But they themselves know they have nothing to fear.

They and the powers they serve will go completely untouched by the imperial murder machine. They will die of old age surrounded by wealth and luxury, completely free from any consequences for their actions.

It was all a sham. Always is. The elections are fake and the game is rigged. The empire will march on completely uninterrupted and entirely unchanged, served by one fraudulent president after the next until its eventual collapse.

Stop buying into the performance. Stop screaming for your favorite political pro wrestler and notice that the blows aren't connecting and the whole match is just a show.

If you want to fight the power, focus your opposition where the real power is. The war machine. Imperial power structures. Intelligence agencies. Plutocracy. Capitalism. Fully unplug your emotional energy from the illusion of electoral politics and dedicate your attention instead to the concrete movements of weapons, resources, and wealth.

As long as they can keep us clapping along with the puppet show, we're never going to pay attention to the forces pulling the strings. We're never going to bring enough awareness to the real problems to find actual solutions and carry them out. We're never going to be able to bring real opposition to real power.

And that's the whole idea. That's why this silly puppet show keeps coming back every four years.

Stop clapping along and start looking around the theater. You know where the empire managers want you to place your attention, so start looking where they don't want you to look.

Wake up.

Featured image is a screenshot from the ABC 10 YouTube channel (Fair Use).

The Face At The Front Desk Changes, The Corporation Remains The Same
•Notes From The Edge Of The Narrative Matrix•

Obama continued and expanded Bush's most evil policies. Trump continued and expanded Obama's most evil policies. Biden continued and expanded Trump's most evil policies. Now Trump is preparing to keep the streak going. The face at the front desk changes, but the corporation stays the same.

•

Trump's insanely pro-Israel cabinet of bloodthirsty Iran hawks suggests that Trump is going to expand the evils of the Biden administration in the middle east. This is a great example of the point I often make that the empire uses Democrats and Republicans the way a boxer uses the jab-cross combo to set up knockout blows.

Democrats and Republicans are different from one another, not in the ways they claim to be different, but in the same way the jab and the cross are used differently in boxing. The jab, thrown with the left hand for an orthodox fighter, is used as a range-finding weapon which can stun or blind the opponent to open them up for a crushing power blow from the right hand. That power blow is called a cross, which is often set up by the jab in the classic "one-two" combination you learn on day one in boxing.

The two parties are not the same, but they are used in conjunction with one another toward the same end, and, most importantly, they are both being used by the same boxer to punch you right in the fucking face. You'll hear people try to argue that Democrats are better because it sometimes hurts less when they're in office, but that's exactly the same as saying it's a good boxing strategy to let your opponent jab you in the face because it hurts less than the cross. You can't understand boxing if you see your opponent's fists as two opposing forces and think you can side with one against the other. You can't understand US politics in that way for the exact same reason.

Any decent boxer will tell you they'd rather fight an opponent with a powerful cross than a masterful jab, because an opponent with a great jab will stifle your offense while allowing their offense to be much more effective — including their cross. The two-armed monster of the US oligarchy will keep using both fists to punch you in the face until you stop staring at its hands and trying to calculate which one you'd rather be smashed by, and start focusing on knocking that motherfucker's head off.

•

Israel regularly bombs buildings full of civilians and then sends sniper drones to go pick off the survivors, including children.

•

It's the most liberal thing ever how Democrats who've been completely ignoring Gaza are pointing to the news of Israeli plans to annex the West Bank and going "HAHAHA see what happens when you stupid Muslims and leftists refuse to support Kamala??"

Like, the West Bank is already an occupied territory. West Bank annexation would have been very escalatory a couple of years ago, but compared to everything that's happened in the last thirteen months it's barely a blip. The way these Democratic Party loyalists spent months frantically telling everyone to shut up about an active genocide are now going "Are you happy now?? Israel's gonna CHANGE THE PAPERWORK on the West Bank!" says so much about their worldview.

•

The only intellectually honest reason to support Trump is because you're a garden variety Republican and you support standard Republican agendas like lower taxes on the rich and low tolerance for human diversity. There is no honest basis to support Trump on antiwar grounds, or because you want the swamp of corruption to be drained from Washington. This was obvious to anyone who paid attention the last time he was president, but it is glaringly obvious now from all the warmongering swamp monsters he's been packing his cabinet with.

This narrative so-called "MAGA Republicans" have about themselves as some new special breed of Republican who are meaningfully different from the Republicans of the past simply is not born out by any kind of material evidence. They're not draining the swamp. They're not fighting the deep state. They're not ending the wars. They're doing all the gross stuff Republicans have always tried to do while LARPing as brave rebels.

I despise the entirety of the Republican Party; it's one of the most evil things humanity has ever produced. But in a sense I actually respect the Republicans who don't pretend to be anything different from what they've always been more than I respect the frauds who pretend they're waging some kind of populist insurgency against the establishment. At least the Ben Shapiros and the Fox News weird hair pundits are honest about who they are and what they're doing.

•

Trump supporters tell me, "At least Trump might end the Ukraine war!"

Trump probably will end the Ukraine war eventually; if he doesn't the next president will. Ukraine has already lost and the US needs its resources to prepare for war with China over Taiwan, so it's only a matter of time before the proxy war is brought to a conclusion. The empire was always going to leave Ukraine a smoldering wreck after a senseless, stupid, insanely dangerous war that could easily have been avoided with a few low-cost concessions and a little diplomacy.

Trumpers have been fixated on Ukraine because it's one of the wars that can be pinned more on the other party (even though Trump himself played a major role in paving the way to that war while he was president), but what matters is what happens after that war ends. Everything about Trump's foreign policy cabinet picks indicates all that war machinery will be redirected toward Iran, China, and who knows where else once Washington stops pretending it's going to help the Ukrainians kick Putin in the balls and retake all their territory. Stop looking for excuses to paint this warmongering empire goon as some kind of antiwar hero and watch what the war machine actually does.

•

The western empire behaves irrationally because it is ultimately run by irrational forces.

The gears of capitalism are turned by the blind pursuit of profit.

Plutocrats and interest groups lobby and bribe in the blind pursuit of power and control.

Empire managers blindly continue the policies and agendas of the previous generation of empire managers, moving war machinery and control mechanisms around the world pursuing planetary domination for its own sake.

And all the individuals running this operation are deeply unconscious people — more unconscious even than the average human — whipped about by forces within themselves that they're not at all aware of like unresolved trauma and maladaptive coping mechanisms.

The empire is flying blind, which is why it looks like it's flying blind. It's why it's doing completely irrational things like destroying the biosphere we all depend on for survival, continuing to work toward global hegemony despite all the evidence that this will fail, continuing to make life harder and harder for the people who live under it despite growing discontent and revolutionary sentiment swelling in the background, and preparing for an unwinnable and self-destructive war with China.

The empire is behaving illogically because it is illogical. The gears are turning themselves. There is ultimately no man behind the curtain, no scheming manipulators unleashing all these evils to advance some grand plot which will benefit them. They're more like bacteria in a petri dish mindlessly consuming the food scientists placed there without slowing down as supplies begin to dwindle. They might have elaborate rationales and narratives to justify why they're doing what they're doing, but ultimately they don't know. They are doing it because they are swept up in the momentum of forces which they do not understand, both internally and externally.

The challenge facing us is to become a conscious species. A species that is responsive rather than reactive, driven not by primitive unconscious impulses and habit but by an alert and truth-based relationship with reality. That's what's being asked of us here in this slice of spacetime. That is the existential hurdle we must find some way to get past. And the western empire is the largest and most concrete manifestation of that obstacle.

Featured image via Trump White House Archived on Flickr (Public Domain).

TRUMP ADDRESSES HATE SPEECH ON COLLEGE CAMPUSES

"America First" Means Stomping Out Free Speech In The US In Order To Help Israel
•Notes From The Edge Of The Narrative Matrix•

There's a video of Donald Trump going around where he says — while standing in front of an Israeli flag — that in his first week in office he's going to stomp out "anti-semitic propaganda" on university campuses throughout the United States. As anyone who's been paying attention knows, this of course means stomping out speech that is critical of Israel and its genocidal atrocities.

This clip has sparked controversy on social media, but the funny thing is it's actually a resurrected older clip from a Trump campaign event back in September. Trump was elected while openly campaigning against free speech, even as his supporters promoted him as a champion of free speech. He campaigned on jailing flag burners as well, for the record.

Trump literally standing before an Israeli flag and vowing to kill free speech for the advancement of Israeli information interests makes a lie of everything the so-called "MAGA movement" has ever claimed to stand for and exposes it for the scam it has always been.

•

Trump supporters are already falling all over themselves to justify his warmongering cabinet picks and his vow to crack down on freedom of assembly on college campuses, and he's not even president yet. These people will put zero pressure on Trump to end wars and fight authoritarianism. They'll bootlick and make excuses throughout the entire four years, just like they did last time. They're not anti-establishment populists, they just want to feel like anti-establishment populists.

I've said it before and I'll say it again: Trump supporters are George W Bush supporters LARPing as Ron Paul supporters.

•

On Thursday The New York Times reported that Elon Musk had met with the Iranian ambassador to the United Nations on behalf of the incoming Trump administration to discuss the possibility of easing tensions in the middle east, much to the delight of Trump supporters everywhere. On Saturday CNN reported that Iran says no meeting took place between its UN ambassador and Elon Musk, and Financial Times reports that the Trump administration is actually set to ramp up aggressions against Iran as soon as Trump takes office.

Trump supporters have been citing the Musk story as evidence that Trump plans to make peace with Iran, and you can expect them to either ignore the Financial Times story or spin it as some 87-D chess maneuver designed to promote "peace through strength".

Anyone who spends their time defending any US president against criticisms of their depraved empire servitude is a pathetic power-worshipping bootlicker. It's an embarrassing, undignified way to live, and Trump apologists should feel bad about it.

•

Love it when something happens that isn't even in the top 100 worst things that have happened to Palestinians in the last 13 months and liberals who've been ignoring Gaza this entire time go I HOPE ALL YOU STUPID LEFTISTS AND MUSLIMS ARE HAPPY WITH YOUR PROTEST VOTE!

•

Kamala Harris: I love Dick Cheney and I own a gun and I hate immigrants and anyone who stands up for Palestinians and I'll be way more hawkish on Iran than Trump.

Liberal pundits: Kamala lost because she went way too woke.

•

Instagram progressive Alexandria Ocasio-Cortez declared on MSNBC that Tulsi Gabbard, Trump's pick for intelligence chief, is "pro-war" despite her efforts to present herself as anti-war.

This is one of those statements that's dishonest when it comes out of the mouth of the person saying it but would be true if someone else said it. It's true that Gabbard is a warmongering genocide apologist who backs all the evil things Biden is doing in the middle east right now, but she's less of a warmonger than the murderous swamp monsters AOC spent the last year endorsing and campaigning for. Gabbard at least promoted diplomacy over war in Ukraine while AOC herself promoted and defended the US proxy war from the word go.

AOC's whole schtick is talking the talk of an anti-imperialist socialist while walking the walk of a standard empire lackey, and this is another good example of this.

•

Everything bad that happens under the Trump administration will have happened because the Democratic Party was too corrupt and evil to run a good campaign with a good platform and a good candidate.

Featured image is a screenshot from NBC News on YouTube (Fair Use).

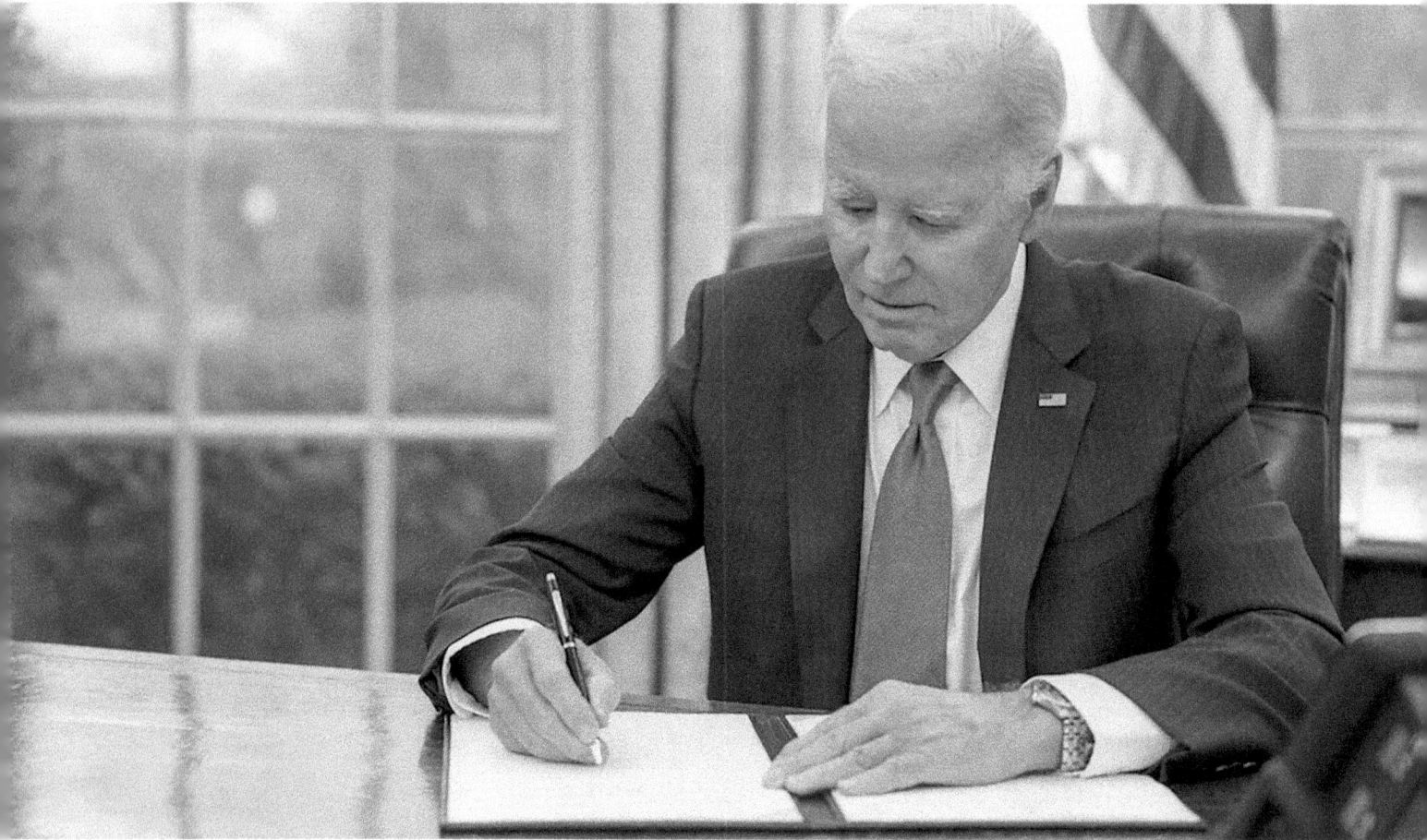

Biden Ramps Up Nuclear Brinkmanship On His Way Out The Door

The New York Times reports that the Biden administration has authorized Ukraine to use US-supplied long-range missiles to strike Russian and North Korean military targets inside Russia — yet another dangerous escalation of nuclear brinkmanship in this horrific proxy war.

The Times correctly notes that authorizing Ukraine to use ATACMS, which have a range of about 190 miles, has long been a contentious issue in the Biden administration for fear of provoking military retaliations against the US from Russia. This reckless escalation has been authorized despite an acknowledgement from the anonymous US officials who spoke to The New York Times that they "do not expect the shift to fundamentally alter the course of the war."

As Antiwar's Dave DeCamp notes, Vladimir Putin said back in September that if NATO allows Ukraine to use western-supplied weapons for long-range strikes inside Russian territory, it would mean NATO countries "are at war with Russia." This is about as unambiguous a threat as you'll ever see.

NYT reports that Biden's policy shift "comes two months before President-elect Donald J. Trump takes office, having vowed to limit further support for Ukraine." And it is here worth noting that last week it was reported by The Telegraph that British PM Keir Starmer and French President Emmanuel Macron had been scheming to thwart any attempt by Trump to scale back US support for Ukraine by pushing Biden to authorize long-range missile strikes in Russian territory.

But it is also true that the day before the US election Mike Waltz, Trump's next national security advisor, had himself endorsed the idea of authorizing long-range missile strikes into Russia with the goal of pressuring Moscow to end the war. His plan for disentangling the US from the conflict entails ramping up sanctions on Russia and "taking the handcuffs off the long-range weapons we provide Ukraine" in order to pressure Putin into eagerly accepting a peace deal.

So while this is being framed as an administration that's more hawkish on Russia executing a maneuver that's designed to hamstring the peacemongering of an incoming administration that's less favorable to assisting Ukraine, in reality it may just be goal-assisting the next administration in a policy change it had planned on implementing anyway.

Either way, it's insane. Putin ordered changes to Russia's nuclear doctrine in September in order to ward off these sorts of escalations by lowering the threshold at which nuclear weapons could be used to defend the Russian Federation, and they're just barreling right past that bright red line like they barreled over the red lines which led to the invasion of Ukraine. And the fact that they're adding yet another nuclear-armed state into the mix with North Korea is just more gravy for the nuclear brinkmanship pot roast.

At one point in 2022, US intelligence agencies reportedly assessed that the odds of Russia using a nuclear weapon in Ukraine was as high as fifty percent, but the Biden administration kept pushing forward with this proxy war anyway. These freaks are taking insane risks to advance agendas that stand to yield the slimmest of benefits even by their own assessments.

We are living in dark and dangerous times.

Featured image via Official White House Photo by Adam Schultz (Public Domain).

Another Psychopath For US Secretary Of State
•Notes From The Edge Of The Narrative Matrix•

Marco Rubio will be joining a long list of psychopaths as the next US secretary of state. A few of Trump's cabinet picks might have a hard time getting past the Senate, but not Rubio. He's the exact type of blood-guzzling swamp leech those creatures on Capitol Hill adore.

Psychopathy is almost a job requirement for secretary of state, because the title entails a responsibility for helping to roll out the violence and tyranny which serves as the glue that holds the US empire together. As secretary of state you are responsible for whipping up international consensus for brutal economic sanctions regimes, drumming up support for heightened aggressions against the official enemies of Washington, and making up excuses for the criminal abuses of the US and its allies.

This is funny in a dark sort of way because the secretary of state is supposed to be in charge of US diplomacy, which in theory should mean making peace and resolving conflicts without violence. The US Department of State was supposed to be the peacemaking counterbalance to the US Department of War (renamed the Department of War was a little too honest), but because the US runs a globe-spanning empire that is held together by endless violence it has little use for peacekeeping, so the State Department mostly gets used to help inflict more violence and abuse. In theory it was supposed to be the Peace Department, but in practice the US just got two War Departments.

Rubio will be a suitable addition to the list of sadistic manipulators who have served in that role before him, joining the likes of Antony Blinken, Mike Pompeo, Hillary Clinton, Madeleine Albright and Henry Kissinger as the next soulless manipulator to lead the US State Department in pressing the imperial boot into the throat of the global south.

•

I've had multiple Kamala supporters angrily tell me I helped Trump win by criticizing Biden's foreign policy in the lead-up to the election. I cannot imagine being so much of an unprincipled bootlicker that I'd expect people to lie about a genocide to help someone win more votes.

•

Nothing Trump will do inside US borders over the next four years will be the tiniest fraction as murderous, tyrannical and worthy of ferocious opposition as what Biden is doing in Gaza right now.

•

American progressives who stopped talking about Gaza in July-August to avoid hurting Kamala seem to have forgotten to go back to talking about Gaza now that the election is over.

•

Trump is profoundly evil, but he is a very conventional kind of profoundly evil, of the same variety as Biden, Obama and Bush before him.

The big lie about Trump is that he is a special deviation from the norm, and both sides believe this lie. Everything about the actual policies of his first term reveal that he is a very ordinary Republican president, who is evil in more or less the same ways as all the other evil Republican presidents. He didn't do anything that wasn't already being done by those before him and won't continue to be done by those after him. But both Democrats and Republicans see him as a drastic departure from status quo US politics, differing only in whether they perceive this as a good thing or a bad thing.

This happens because US presidents cannot significantly differ from one another in actual policy and decision making. If they were the sort to disrupt the status quo too much, they never would have been allowed to ascend to the presidency. There is simply too much power riding on the US empire for any significant change in its operations to be tolerated by the actual power structure which really runs things. So because presidents and viable presidential candidates cannot significantly differ from each other in terms of policy, they instead differ from each other in terms of narrative and emotion.

That's what we're seeing in all the vitriol and passion and frenetic punditry about Trump on both sides of the US partisan divide. A bunch of empty narrative fluff pouring a lot of emotional energy into either supporting or opposing a very ordinary evil in a very ordinary Republican president.

If they didn't do that, the entire US political landscape would just be Democrats and Republicans agreeing with one another about 99 percent of the evils of the US empire and half-heartedly disagreeing about the remaining one percent. And that would give the whole game away. It would kill the illusion that Americans live in a real democracy where their votes actually mean something and they actually have some meaningful degree of control over what their government does. If this understanding took root, it would only be a matter of time until America's heavily-armed population began thinking thoughts of revolution.

So we're left watching these ridiculous histrionics over what amounts to the ordinary everyday pendulum swings between ordinary everyday Democrat governance and ordinary everyday Republican governance, with one side remaining in control about half the time and both sides working together to push the status quo further and further into oligarchy, militarism and tyranny.

The whole US political spectacle is all emotion and no substance. A tale told by an idiot, full of sound and fury, signifying nothing.

Featured image via Gage Skidmore (CC BY-SA 2.0)

Who Is Authorizing Biden's Nuclear Brinkmanship While The President's Brain Is Missing?
•Notes From The Edge Of The Narrative Matrix•

Ukraine has already begun using US-supplied long-range missiles in Russia, despite Putin's warning that this exact sort of escalation will place NATO at war with Russia. This happens as Russia officially changes its nuclear doctrine to lower the threshold for when it's permissible to use nuclear weapons in retaliation for attacks on its territory.

So far the attacks appear to have been mostly repelled without having done any significant damage.

This is frightening, but I have a hard time imagining that Russia makes any extreme moves against the US before Trump takes office. It seems like they'd want to wait and see what Trump does once he gets in before taking any horrifying risks like that. It is much more likely that Russia will instead respond to this escalation by escalating its attacks on Ukraine, like it normally does.

Who knows, though? If these attacks on Russia continue, there's literally no limit to how bad this could get.

•

It's so fun how the Biden administration is using its lame duck months to skyrocket hostilities between nuclear superpowers and we don't even know who's really making these decisions because the president's brain is cottage cheese.

•

These escalations happen as Ukrainians begin moving into a majority consensus that it is time to seek peace. A new Gallup poll has found that a majority of Ukrainians throughout the country now support peace talks to end the war with Russia, with 52 percent favoring peace and 38 percent wanting to fight on.

As usual people are more opposed to continuing the war the closer they are to the frontline, with 63 percent of the respondents in eastern Ukraine supporting peace talks and only 27 percent wanting to continue fighting. The further you are from the effects of this horrific proxy war the more likely you are to support it; it's just as true inside Ukraine's borders as it is when you include all the western armchair warriors who want to continue fighting to the last Ukrainian.

"Listen to the Ukrainians," we were told when all this started. Well, here they are. This proxy war has been waged in the name of defending Ukrainian democracy, and yet it continues to dangerously escalate against the will of the majority, at the direction of a president in Kyiv whose elected term ended months ago.

•

Fighting a war with Russia always seems like a swell idea until you actually try it. The fact that the majority of Ukrainians now support ending the war is yet another example of this oft-repeated history lesson.

•

The only way to view Trump as significantly worse than Biden is to take very little interest US foreign policy, and the only way to take so little interest in US foreign policy is to care very little about non-western lives.

•

Every day I'm interacting with liberals who inadvertently reveal that they are only just now beginning to pay close attention to what's happening in Gaza, now that they'll be able to blame the genocide on someone else. I was just talking to a Democrat who informed me I'm going to miss Biden after hundreds of Palestinians begin starving to death in Gaza when Trump gets into office. I told him Palestinians are believed to be starving to death by the tens of thousands presently; we just don't hear about it because indirect deaths like malnutrition aren't part of the official daily death toll.

It's so much worse than they realize because they spent more than a year looking the other way while it was happening, so now you'll often see them warning that Trump is going to do things that Biden has been doing this entire time.

•

People who say you get more conservative as you get older are just projecting their own personal shittiness onto everyone else. I get more radicalized by the year. It's not even about older people having more wealth to protect; I'm making more money than ever before and I still want to obliterate capitalism.

You get more conservative and right wing as you get older if you fail to grow as you age. It just means you've been wasting your time on this planet and allowing yourself to become intellectually lazy and morally stagnant.

Featured image is an official White House Photo by Adam Schultz.

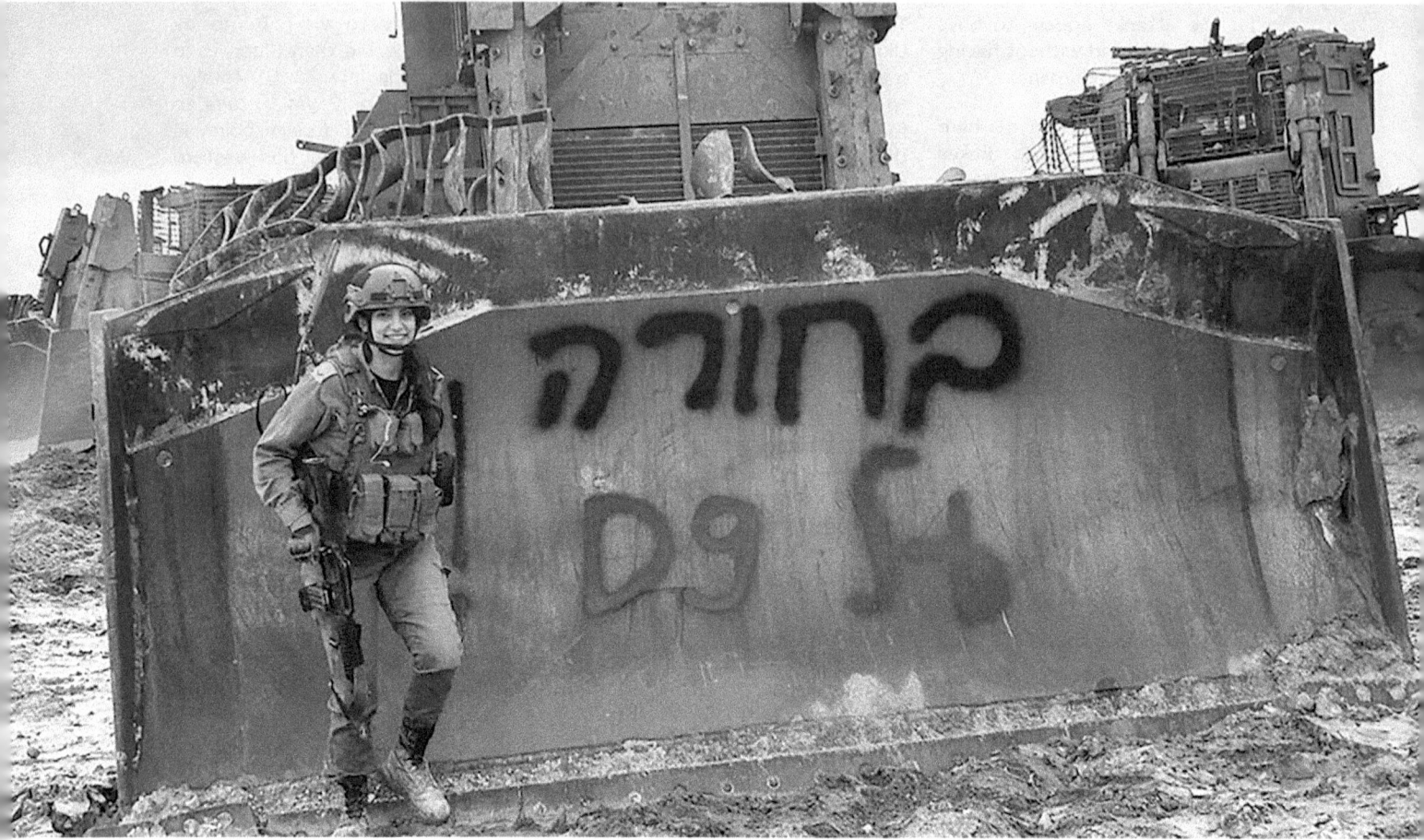

The Real Israel

One of the very few good things coming out of the relentless nightmare happening in Gaza is that at long last the western world is getting a clear look at Israel. The real Israel.

Not the Israel they teach you about in school. Not "the only democracy in the middle east," where Jews were given safe haven after their victimization at the hands of the Nazis and managed to create a thriving society despite existing in a sea of savage enemies bent on their destruction.

Not that Israel. The real one. Arguably the most racist society on earth, whose existence has depended on nonstop violence, theft, tyranny and abuse since its very inception.

The real Israel, whose government is deliberately and methodically starving Palestinian civilians to death by the tens of thousands just for being the wrong ethnicity.

The real Israel, whose snipers routinely murders Palestinian children by shooting them in the head.

The real Israel, whose military is so sadistic that it created an AI system to specifically target suspected Hamas fighters when they are at home with their families, and called the AI "Where's Daddy?" because it would be killing fathers when they are at home with their children.

The real Israel, whose soldiers cannot stop posting footage of themselves mockingly dressed in the undergarments of dead and displaced Palestinian women and playing with the toys of dead and displaced Palestinian children.

The real Israel, where Palestinian doctors are raped and tortured to death.

The real Israel, where the majority of men do not believe acquaintance rape or spousal rape are real crimes, and where the majority do not believe the soldiers accused of raping and torturing a Palestinian prisoner to the point of severe injury should face criminal charges.

The real Israel, who routinely bombs buildings full of civilians and then uses sniper drones to pick off the survivors, including children.

The real Israel, whose drones have been heard playing the sounds of crying babies and screaming women in order to lure out civilians so they can be killed.

The real Israel, who has damaged or destroyed 94 percent of the healthcare facilities in Gaza with hundreds of targeted attacks.

The real Israel, whose military forces target medical staff so methodically that doctors and nurses in Gaza reportedly change out of their uniforms when they leave the hospital in order to avoid assassination.

The real Israel, who hates truth so much that it has been killing historic numbers of journalists in Gaza while preventing foreign journalists from entering the enclave.

The real Israel, who has been knowingly attacking the locations of humanitarian aid workers.

The real Israel, whose citizens are so warped and twisted that they attend boat tours to cheerfully witness the devastation in the Gaza Strip.

The real Israel, whose citizens set up blockades to prevent aid trucks from getting to starving civilians in Gaza while they enjoy barbecues and set up bouncy castles and cotton candy machines for their children.

The real Israel, whose TikTok influencers started a viral trend mocking the suffering of civilians in Gaza.

The real Israel, whose citizens will travel to another country and tear down Palestinian flags and sing about how there are no children left in Gaza and then cry victim when people fight back.

This is the real Israel, in all its glory. And it is good that it is being seen.

The sooner everyone stops supporting this freakish, murderous society and begins insisting that normal human values win out over the demented forces which keep it going, the sooner there can be peace in the region. And the better off our entire species will be.

Featured image via Wikimedia Commons/IDF.

Today In Imperial Recklessness And Insanity

The International Criminal Court has formally issued arrest warrants for Israeli Prime Minister Benjamin Netanyahu and former Israeli Defense Minister Yoav Gallant for war crimes and crimes against humanity.

No such arrest warrants were issued for President Biden or any of the other western officials who've been backing Israel's genocidal atrocities, which is a bit like a judge issuing a warrant for a mass murderer but not for the guy who gave him the gun and stood next to him handing him ammunition and drove the getaway car and lied to the police to cover up the crime.

Nothing will come of this new development because it is completely unenforcible and international law is only as real as the US empire agrees to pretend it is, but it is a significant step in the deterioration of international consensus on Israel as the entire world watches the Zionist regime commit atrocity after atrocity right out in the open.

Predictably, Benjamin Netanyahu has responded to this decision by shrieking about antisemitism and calling the ICC's move "a modern Dreyfus trial". He is doing this because he does not have anything resembling a real argument in his defense, and neither does anyone else.

We saw this illustrated in a statement from Senator Tom Cotton, who proclaimed that the US would invade The Hague if the ICC tries to enforce its arrest warrants.

"The ICC is a kangaroo court and Karim Khan is a deranged fanatic," Cotton said. "Woe to him and anyone who tries to enforce these outlaw warrants. Let me give them all a friendly reminder: the American law on the ICC is known as The Hague Invasion Act for a reason. Think about it."

This is as psychotic a public statement as anything you'll see from the most far-right extremists in the Knesset. The United States is run by demented zealots with nukes, just like Israel.

The "Hague Invasion Act", formally known as the American Service-Members' Protection Act, is a US federal law passed during the warmongering frenzy of the early Bush administration which authorizes the president to use "all means necessary and appropriate to bring about the release of any U.S. or allied personnel being detained or imprisoned by, on behalf of, or at the request of the International Criminal Court."

That "or allied personnel" bit is why Cotton is able to cite this law in reference to an arrest warrant for Israelis.

Speaking of Israel and US senators, a bill by Bernie Sanders to block a shipment of tank shells to Israel was just killed in the Senate by a vote of 18 to 79.

Sanders framed the bill as an effort to restrict "the sale of offensive arms to Israel", making a distinction from "defensive" arms like the Iron Dome, which is absurd and obfuscatory to begin with. All arms to Israel are offensive rather than defensive in nature, in that they are all used to help Israel murder people without experiencing the deterrence they would receive from a retaliatory response. There's a reason body armor is regulated in a way that's similar to firearms; it's because someone who wants to commit a violent crime can wear a bulletproof vest while doing so to ensure that they can perpetrate the crime without being stopped by police. That's exactly how Israel uses its so-called "defensive" weaponry.

And speaking of progressive US lawmakers taking feeble stands on Israel, congresswoman Alexandria Ocasio-Cortez has come under fire for voting to support House Resolution 1449, a bill which purports to simply denounce antisemitism but in reality promotes the false conflation of antisemitic hate speech with speech that is critical of Israel.

Progressive congresswoman Ilhan Omar, who voted against the bill, said in a statement that she did so because "the bill endorses the harmful definition of IHRA that dangerously conflates legitimate criticism of Israel to antisemitism and further harms our ability to address antisemitism."

Everywhere you look it's powerful criminals getting away with far too much while the people who are supposed to be resisting them do far too little.

This happens as Russia hits Ukraine with a new type of hypersonic missile, which Putin went out of his way to mention could easily have been equipped with a nuclear warhead. This attack was a warning to Ukraine for using long-range missiles supplied by the US and UK to strike targets inside Russia, and occurs as Moscow revises its nuclear doctrine lowering the threshold for when nuclear weapons may be used.

This is unsustainable. It cannot continue. One way or the other, all this madness is going to come to an end.

Featured image via Hudson Institute (CC BY 2.0)

If You Want To Help The World, Focus On Fighting The Empire

Become a soldier because you want to be of service and you will discover that being a soldier doesn't work the way it's depicted in movies and shows. You're not a hero defending your country from murderous thugs, you are the murderous thugs, and the people you are murdering are trying to defend their country from you.

Become a cop because you want to be of service and you will discover that being a cop doesn't work the way it's depicted in movies and shows. Your job isn't to protect people from crime, your job is to protect a system whose very existence is criminal, and none of the worst people in your society ever go to prison.

Become a lawyer because you want to be of service and you will discover that being a lawyer doesn't work the way it's depicted in movies and shows. The laws aren't there to protect ordinary people from the worst among us, they are there to protect the worst among us from ordinary people.

Become a politician because you want to be of service and you will discover that being a politician doesn't work the way it's depicted in movies and shows. The power and influence you can wield in politics is directly proportionate to your willingness to compromise and collaborate with the plutocrats, interest groups and power structures who are causing the very problems you're trying to solve in the first place.

Become a journalist because you want be of service and you will discover that being a journalist doesn't work the way it's depicted in movies and shows. The job of the media in your society are not to report the truth and hold power to account but to propagandize the citizenry into accepting status quo politics and consenting to acts of mass military slaughter around the world, and you can only rise to success in the press to the extent that you are willing to help generate that propaganda.

Become a teacher because you want be of service and you will discover that being a teacher doesn't work the way it's depicted in movies and shows. As a teacher your job is to lie to the next generation about their nation, their government, their history and their world and indoctrinate them into trusting their government and news media.

Become a therapist because you want be of service and you will discover that being a therapist doesn't work the way it's depicted in movies and shows. A huge amount of the anxiety and depression your clients bring you cannot be resolved in therapy because they arise from the poverty, toil and lack of support which is built into the abusive and exploitative society in which we live.

Become a social worker because you want be of service and you will discover that being a social worker doesn't work the way it's depicted in movies and shows. Again and again you will fail to secure your clients the resources they desperately need because your government doesn't care about them and your society flushes anyone who can't be used to generate a profit down the toilet.

Try to make movies and shows which tell the truth about the kind of society we live in, and you will discover that the only way movies and shows get produced and placed before a large audience is if they promote the class interests of the wealthy people who control the major studios and platforms. Hollywood is one giant propaganda service for empire and capitalism.

We live in a civilization built of lies and abuse, powered by lies and abuse, and defended using lies and abuse. Even the most kindhearted and well-intentioned among us struggle to bring about positive change, because the very fabric of our society is stacked against truth and kindness.

Do you wish to be of service? Do you want to help the world? Then focus your energy on fighting against the status quo power structure which makes it so difficult to serve and to help. Do everything you can to help foment a revolutionary zeitgeist in opposition to militarism, capitalism, imperialism, authoritarianism, and the mainstream politics and media which make these abuses possible.

Work on opening people's eyes to the lies and abuse which sustain the tyrannical power structure we all live under, and open their hearts to the possibility that it doesn't need to be this way. The more eyes and hearts are opened in this way, the closer the people get to using the power of their numbers to force the emergence of a healthy world.

Featured image via Adobe Stock.

Only A Truth–Based Relationship With Reality Can Satisfy

What we all want, deep down, is a truth-based relationship with reality. We might not be aware that this is what we are seeking from life, but it is. And everything in our society is stacked against our ever getting it.

Everything in our society tells us to orient ourselves toward falsehood. Toward the lies of the empire. Toward the gratification of the ego. Toward fraudulent strategies for happiness which can never, ever satisfy. And all we really want deep down is truth.

The overwhelming majority of humanity is lost in delusion. Our minds are full of propaganda-induced hallucinations about a completely fictional world in which capitalism is working just fine and the US and its allies stand on the side of freedom and justice. Our behavior is driven by advertising and cultural indoctrination about what we should buy and how hard we should work to buy it and what kinds of goals we should be striving to achieve. Our psyches are wrapped around a believed sense of self which is completely and utterly illusory.

We flail this way and that seeking happiness and satisfaction from sources which can never provide them to us, because they aren't true. We buy all the products we're told to buy and find they yield only the most shallow and fleeting sort of enjoyment. We chase all the goals we're told to chase and then find ourselves in a mid-life crisis when we're still miserable after spending decades successfully achieving them. We try to find some inner stability by obtaining knowledge about the world and find ourselves fighting off cognitive dissonance because of the contradictions between the propaganda-induced mainstream consensus about reality and the raw data of what's actually going on.

We are unhappy because we live in a civilization made of lies, but because we live in a civilization made of lies, everything we reach for in an effort to escape our unhappiness is itself made of lies. Buy this product. Become fit enough and beautiful enough. Become wealthy and impressive. Fill your head with knowledge from all the most respected and esteemed sources. Happiness is just around the corner if you can only obtain the next shiny thing.

It's all lies. It cannot satisfy.

The only thing that can satisfy is a truth-based relationship with reality. One in which your worldview is in alignment with truth, and your thoughts are in alignment with your worldview, and your words are in alignment with your thoughts, and your deeds are in alignment with your words.

Happiness and satisfaction are not the result of getting everything you want and becoming the envy of the town, happiness and satisfaction are the result of purging your mind of falsehood. Falsehood about the world and the way it works. Falsehood about your life and your relationships. Falsehood about yourself and your true nature.

There are many different ways we can delude ourselves, and it's possible to be fairly free of delusion in one respect but deeply deluded in others. Someone who's spent a long time researching global power dynamics and abusive systems might have a lucid understanding of the ways in which the rich and powerful conspire against the interests of ordinary people, but be totally enslaved to their ego and harbor countless unquestioned false beliefs about reality. Someone who's spent decades in meditation and contemplation may have seen through the delusions of self and separation, but still harbor a deeply unconscious perspective on the world that's not much different from what you'll see pundits spewing on Fox News or CNN.

The extent to which we experience satisfaction is the extent to which we stand against untruth. Untruth in ourselves, untruth in our immediate community, and untruth in the world. This necessarily entails a courageous willingness to look directly at very ugly things in all of those areas.

Anyone who sincerely resolves to get real about reality will at some point find themselves staring at some dark, ugly things inside themselves that they wish weren't there. But the first step to healing ourselves of untruth is to get real about the untruth that's hiding in the shadows of our subconscious.

Anyone who sincerely resolves to get real about reality will likewise find themselves staring at dark, ugly facts which contradict the mainstream worldview we've all been indoctrinated into mistaking for truth. The genocide in Gaza has been one long, uninterrupted lesson in how profoundly ugly these truths can be.

We will never have a healthy world until we are capable of becoming a truth-driven species. A species driven not by propaganda and the fraudulent psychological delusions of fear, greed, hatred and self-interest, but by truth and sincerity. I am firmly convinced that we are capable of becoming such a species.

The cool thing about this is that the journey in this direction begins right beneath our own two feet. Right here in this moment you can get curious about what's true, and where untruth may be hiding in your beliefs and assumptions about yourself, others, and the world. Human delusion runs profoundly deep, so every one of us has some untruth lurking around in the background which can be drawn into consciousness and healed.

Remove all untruth from yourself, and do everything you can to remove untruth from the world around you. This is what a truth-driven life looks like. And it's how we begin the work of building a truth-driven world.

Featured image via Adobe Stock.

DNIPRO, UKRAINE
THURSDAY

FORMER
SUNDAY

MIKE WALTZ [R]

Trump's Cabinet Picks Aren't Looking Good For Peace In Ukraine

Conventional wisdom about the outgoing Biden administration's reckless escalations in Ukraine these past few days is that things will cool down once Donald Trump takes office, but Trump's cabinet picks aren't really selling this idea.

While Trump did campaign on ending the war in Ukraine, the president elect has given multiple cabinet appointments to strategists who say that the way to achieve that peace is to substantially escalate aggressions against Russia. Michael Tracey has been doing a great job compiling footage of Trump's recent cabinet picks advocating extreme measures which happen to be in perfect alignment with the nuclear brinkmanship of the demented outgoing president and his handlers.

Sebastian Gorka, who Trump has named as his next senior director for counterterrorism, is on record saying that Trump has told him he plans on saying to Putin, "You will negotiate now or the aid that we have given to Ukraine thus far will look like peanuts."

Mike Waltz, who Trump has selected as his next national security advisor, promotes a similar vision. Waltz says Russia can be pressured to come to the negotiating table via increased energy sanctions combined with "taking the handcuffs off of the long-range weapons we provided Ukraine." Biden has since removed those very "handcuffs" by authorizing Kyiv to use US-supplied long-range missiles to attack Russia.

If it seems like these remarks from Trump's incoming administration work very nicely with the actions of the outgoing administration, then you may find it interesting that Waltz just told Fox News Sunday that the two administrations are working "hand in glove" as the presidency changes over.

"Jake Sullivan and I have had discussions, we've met," Waltz said. "For our adversaries out there that think this is a time of opportunity, that they can play one administration off the other — they are wrong. We are hand in glove. We are one team with the United States in this transition."

This would seem to be an oblique reference to Russia specifically, since that's the only US adversary with any hope that the incoming administration might be a bit less hawkish toward it than the outgoing one, and since years of mass media coverage went into spinning narratives about Trump being a pawn of Vladimir Putin.

But Trump was never a pawn of Vladimir Putin. Contrary to the narratives of both Democrat-aligned punditry and Republican-aligned punditry while he was in office, Trump spent his entire term ramping up cold war aggressions against Russia which helped pave the way to the war and brinkmanship we are seeing in Ukraine today. Tracey

recently shared an audio clip of Gorka on X Spaces back in January 2023 exuberantly boasting about the way Trump ordered the US military to kill hundreds of Russian mercenaries in Syria in 2018. Putin himself cited the Trump administration's withdrawal from the Intermediate-Range Nuclear Forces treaty in 2019 when defending his decision to hit Ukraine with a new type of intermediate-range missile the other day in response to its use of US- and UK-supplied long-range missiles to strike inside Russia.

Other cabinet appointments who have taken extremely hawkish positions on Russia include secretary of state nominee Marco Rubio, secretary of defense nominee Pete Hegseth, CIA director nominee John Ratcliffe, and National Security Council appointee Doug Burgum. But it's those comments from Waltz and Gorka which I find most concerning, because they explicitly refer to escalatory strategies that Trump might employ once he takes office.

This all comes out as we get news that US and European officials recently discussed providing nuclear weapons to Ukraine under the gamble that Putin will not escalate against the west before Trump takes office. The more aligned the Trump administration's posture toward Russia appears to be with that of the Biden administration, the less safe a gamble this appears to be.

It seems likely that the Trump administration will end the Ukraine proxy war at some point down the road in order to reallocate those resources toward preparation for war with Iran and/or China. But it is not at all clear that this will happen soon enough before soaring escalations spin out of control into the single worst-case scenario that could possibly unfold on this planet.

Featured image is a screenshot from Fox News on YouTube (Fair Use).

In The Fight Against Tyranny, Don't Let Your Happiness Depend On Big Wins

If you stand for truth, peace and justice in this world then it's important not to make your happiness dependent on large-scale wins.

Because the deck is stacked so heavily against truth, peace and justice, your side will experience far more losses than wins. You will watch powerlessly as your government backs genocides, starts wars, and unleashes nightmare after nightmare upon the global south. Your heroes will disappoint you. Your protest movements will fizzle. Your civil rights will erode, your speech will be marginalized, the wealthy and powerful will amass more wealth and power while the poor and the powerless grow ever more so.

I say this not as an expression of pessimism or defeatism, but because that's simply where we're at as a society right now. Ours is a highly controlled dystopia where minds are continuously inundated with power-serving propaganda and tyrants enact their abusive agendas without much meaningful resistance. This doesn't mean we can't win, it just means we can't realistically expect many big wins in the immediate future under our current circumstances while truth has so much difficulty getting a word in edgewise.

You can let all the human suffering depress you and let all your failed attempts to stop it drag you down, or you can look to some other source for your happiness which isn't dependent on securing large-scale wins for humanity.

For me this is a no-brainer. It does nobody any good for me to be miserable all the time, and in fact letting myself get bogged down in depression and despair would make my efforts a lot less prolific and effective. A dissident voice choosing to be unhappy just because there's so much suffering in the world would be like a revolutionary soldier choosing to be weak and emaciated and worthless on the battlefield just because there are so many people who are starving. A happy mind is a healthy mind, a healthy mind is an effective mind, and we need our minds to be as effective as possible while we work to awaken our civilization from the lies of the empire.

So don't bind your happiness to the success of your efforts. As Chris Hedges has said, "I do not fight fascists because I will win. I fight fascists because they are fascists." Do everything you can to fight back against the lies, war and tyranny of the empire, but do it for its own sake because it's the right thing to do, not because you've wrapped up your sense of wellbeing in the success of failure of your fight.

Instead, find your happiness elsewhere. In your love for your fellow humans. In the jaw-dropping beauty of this miraculous planet we get to live on. In the raw enjoyment of feeling the air in your lungs and the ground beneath your feet. In being present in the senses rather than immersed in the dull repetitive chatter of the mind.

Happiness is a skill that can be learned with practice, and it is worthwhile to learn that skill. The revolution doesn't need a bunch of despondent, burnt-out minds, it needs vibrant minds full of zest for life on this planet, who really have something to fight for.

By not allowing yourself to be happy, you're not helping the needful, you're just depriving the world of that much happiness. Any joy you can allow into your life will have beneficial knock-on effects on every life you touch, and any joy you shut out will deprive them of that.

And you deserve to be happy. You do. If this feels untrue to you, the happiness is hiding just beneath that feeling. See if you can get underneath it and unhook whatever beliefs are binding you to that pointless, unhelpful fixation. You are worthy of happiness and inner peace.

Find your happiness and continue to fight ferociously, without placing too much importance on whether your efforts will succeed or fail today. All we can do is keep throwing our own little bit of sand into the gears of the machine, knowing that one day, with enough sand, the whole thing will start grinding to a halt.

There's no good reason to waste our time on this earth depriving ourselves of happiness in the meantime.

Featured image via Adobe Stock.